MW00478864

# Cambridge Elements ᐀

Elements in Quantitative and Computational
Methods for Social Science
R. Michael Alvarez
*California Institute of Technology*
and
Nathaniel Beck
*NYU*

# TWITTER AS DATA

## Zachary C. Steinert-Threlkeld
*University of California, Los Angeles*

CAMBRIDGE
UNIVERSITY PRESS

# CAMBRIDGE
## UNIVERSITY PRESS

University Printing House, Cambridge CB2 8BS, United Kingdom

One Liberty Plaza, 20th Floor, New York, NY 10006, USA

477 Williamstown Road, Port Melbourne, VIC 3207, Australia

314–321, 3rd Floor, Plot 3, Splendor Forum, Jasola District Centre, New Delhi – 110025, India

79 Anson Road, #06–04/06, Singapore 079906

Cambridge University Press is part of the University of Cambridge.

It furthers the University's mission by disseminating knowledge in the pursuit of education, learning, and research at the highest international levels of excellence.

www.cambridge.org
Information on this title: www.cambridge.org/9781108438339
DOI: 10.1017/9781108529327

First published 2018

*A catalogue record for this publication is available from the British Library.*

ISBN 978-1-108-43833-9 Paperback
ISSN 2398-4023 (Online)
ISSN 2514-3794 (Print)

1

# Twitter As Data

Zachary C. Steinert-Threlkeld*

**Abstract:** *The rise of the internet and mobile telecommunications has created the possibility of using large datasets to understand behavior at unprecedented levels of temporal and geographic resolution. Online social networks attract the most users, though users of these new technologies provide their data through multiple sources, e.g. call detail records, blog posts, web forums, and content aggregation sites. These data allow scholars to adjudicate between competing theories as well as develop new ones, much as the microscope facilitated the development of the germ theory of disease. Of those networks, Twitter presents an ideal combination of size, international reach, and data accessibility that make it the preferred platform in academic studies. Acquiring, cleaning, and analyzing these data, however, require new tools and processes. This Element introduces these methods to social scientists and provides scripts and examples for downloading, processing, and analyzing Twitter data. All data and code for this Element is available at www.cambridge.org/twitter-as-data*

**Keywords:** *Twitter; political science; computational social science; CSS; social science; big data; NLP; natural language processing; data science*

**Issns:** 2398-4023 (Online), 2514-3794 (Print)
**Isbns:** 9781108438339 PB, 9781108529327 OC

## 1 Twitter

The increasing prevalence of digital communications technology – the internet and mobile phones – provides the possibility of analyzing human behavior at a level of detail previously unimaginable.

* Department of Public Policy, University of California, Los Angeles, CA
To whom correspondence should be addressed: zst@luskin.ucla.edu

Blogs, content aggregation sites, internet fora, online social networks, and call data records provide access to data that vary by the second. For political scientists interested in questions about elections, language, political communication, conflict, or spatial diffusion, among others, the rise of these technologies holds much promise (Grimmer and Stewart, 2013; Bail, 2014).

These data require new tools to acquire, process, and, sometimes, analyze. These tools are no more difficult to learn and use than other qualitative and quantitative methods, but they are not commonly taught to social scientists. There also exists no canonical text, in journal or book form, that explains the strengths and weaknesses of these data and tools. This Element provides a systematic introduction to these data sources and the tools needed to benefit from them.

While digital communications technology provides data through numerous platforms, I focus on one, the social network Twitter. With over 300 million accounts creating 500 million messages per day, it is one of the largest social networks. Its data are also relatively easy to access, unlike Facebook's. While other social media platforms and websites also facilitate data access, none is as general purpose as Twitter. Twitter's global reach, large user base, and data openness make it the preferred platform for large-scale studies of human behavior.

I use the Twitter behavior of 21 accounts from Egypt and Bahrain as a running example. Nineteen of these accounts belong to civil society actors from four different social movements, and two belong to the Bahraini government. I detail how to purchase their tweets, download their old tweets, download specific tweets based on a unique tweet identifier, download their new tweets as they are created, and analyze these tweets. Analysis will focus on textual and spatial analysis; for an explanation of network analysis using Twitter, see Steinert-Threlkeld (2016). Throughout these examples, I provide full working code as well as any data necessary.

The rest of this Element is divided into a further five sections. Section 2 explains where to acquire Twitter data for your research. You can download the data yourself through the REST API or streaming API (see the glossary for a definition of REST, API, and other acronyms.) The REST API is for finding user metadata, account relationships, and old tweets. The streaming API is for downloading data in real time. You can purchase them, or you can work with a collaborator who has obtained data that matches your research interests.

Section 3 details how to acquire Twitter data from the REST API and streaming API. It starts with creating a Twitter account, which is necessary to access the API. It then provides code for the most common data needs: downloading a user's tweets, downloading specific tweets, finding tweets, or downloading lists of an account's followers and the accounts a specific account follows. The section also shows how to connect to the streaming API for a random sample. The streaming API accepts parameters for language, keywords, accounts, and places, and the section shows how to use those as well. It then finishes with a discussion of different data storage approaches.

Section 4 shows how to conduct common analyses on data acquired via the methods in Sections 2 and 3. Processing is required to move from raw tweets to tweets in rectangular format. The section then shows how to conduct text analysis using tweets and detect real-world events from them. It also discusses possibilities of image analysis and generating metadata for a tweet, such as demographic information.

Section 5 discusses how social scientists have used Twitter to date. Only in the last five years have scholars started to incorporate Twitter into quantitative analyses. Work has focused on using Twitter to measure conflict dynamics, social networks, political preferences, legislative responsiveness, economic outcomes, and mobilization for contentious action. The section also discusses social media platforms, such as Facebook and Instagram, and explains why Twitter is likely to remain the dominant source of social network data for social scientists.

Section 6 concludes with several discussions of Twitter as a data source. The section discusses limits to acquiring data and making inferences given the little information provided in individual tweets. It discusses potential ethical concerns with tweets, especially around protected groups of people such as children. Finally, it concludes that Twitter exhibits characteristics of a media platform and social network, meaning social scientists can use it to study both media, elite individuals, and normal people.

## 1.1   Why Twitter?

Six features of Twitter have driven its popularity for academic study. First, it is one of the largest social networks, with 319 million monthly active users from almost every country and over $1 billion of annual revenue (Twitter, 2016). These users include heads of state, companies, non-profit organizations, international non-governmental organizations, celebrities, athletes, journalists, academics, and, primarily, normal people. In the United States, as of November 2016, 24% of adults use Twitter; men and women use it equally, a plurality of users are between 18 and 29 years of age (a majority, 18–49), a plurality of users have at least a college degree (20% have a high school degree or less), a majority earn more than $50,000 per year, and users are evenly distributed across urban, suburban, and rural areas. Forty-two percent of its users use it daily and 24% at least once a week (versus 76% and 15% for Facebook) (Greenwood *et al.*, 2016). Twitter therefore provides a cross-section of almost any group in which a researcher would find interest.

Second, users produce copious data, 500 million messages per day. All these people and messages mean that Twitter mirrors vast segments of the population that would otherwise require large teams of researchers to analyze concurrently. Taken together, these first two characteristics mean that almost any event is recorded on Twitter, and many events are predictable as a result of it. For literature on event prediction using Twitter, see Table 1 at the end of Section 1.2.

Third, it makes these data relatively easy to obtain. Twitter provides users' data through two APIs, the streaming API and the REST API, that are accessible to anyone with a Twitter account. Before the switch to v1.1 of the APIs, Twitter allowed third parties to provide interfaces that allowed individuals with no programming experience to access its APIs. Now, that

**Table 1** Twitter literature

| Topic | Reference |
| --- | --- |
| Prediction | Box office (Asur and Huberman, 2010) |
| | Coups (Kallus, 2013) |
| | Crime (Gerber, 2014) |
| | Memes (Garcia-Herranz *et al.*, 2014) |
| | Stock market (Bollen *et al.*, 2011; Zheludev *et al.*, 2014) |
| | Unrest (Ramakrishnan *et al.*, 2014; Steinert-Threlkeld, 2017b) |
| Disaster Response | Starbird and Palen, 2010; Vieweg *et al.*, 2010; Yardi and Boyd, 2010 |
| Polarization | Barberá *et al.*, 2015a; Borge-Holthoefer, *et al.*, 2015 |
| Congress | Barberá *et al.*, 2014; Anastasopoulos *et al.*, 2016 |
| Demographics | Hale *et al.*, 2011; Zamal *et al.*, 2012; Mocanu *et al.*, 2013 |
| Economics | Acemoglu *et al.*, 2014; Llorente *et al.*, 2014 |
| Geography | Yardi and Boyd, 2010; Kulshrestha *et al.*, 2012; Conover *et al.*, 2013; Frank *et al.*, 2013 |
| Sentiment | Dodds *et al.*, 2011; Golder and Macy, 2011. |

capability no longer exists, raising the barrier to entry for acquiring data. Nonetheless, because of Twitter's popularity, there are a large number of software libraries to access Twitter, including in Python and R. You need some programming knowledge to interact with the APIs, though not as much as just a few years ago. The primary purpose of this Element is to help the reader gain that knowledge.

Fourth, the APIs make it easy to tailor the data received to a specific research question. You can receive as much as 1% of all tweets every day (from the streaming API) or filter the tweets received based on keywords, user location, user IDs, or language used. Through the REST API, you can download specific tweets, 3,200 of a user's most recent tweets, a list of who a user follows or who follows the user, and user profile information. In other words, though Twitter has pioneered many "big data" technologies, you do not necessarily need to possess these skills to access Twitter's data. You may need to learn new skills to gather the data, but modeling and visualizing those data can be done with old tools of the trade.

Fifth, Twitter is an excellent data source for network and non-network analysis. Since the service is explicitly structured as a network – connections between accounts are the fundamental building blocks of the user experience – researchers interested in diffusion processes and emergent behavior find Twitter a natural resource. But Twitter, because its 1% stream delivers tweets without information on the tweet author's social network, is also a compelling source for researchers interested in polling and event prediction (Gayo-Avello, 2013).

Sixth, Twitter has a norm of public conversation that does not exist on Facebook. While Facebook also provides an API, most users choose not to make their information publicly available. To gain access to a private user's information, you need to design a Facebook app that the user installs, or work with Facebook's research team. This team maintains veto power over research proposals and publications, and the recent controversy over manipulation of Facebook feeds has caused Facebook to tighten control over its research team (Kramer *et al.*, 2014).

## 1.2   Types of Questions

Twitter data can be used to answer questions that involve three kinds of data: networks, text, and spatial.

Perhaps the most exciting potential of Twitter is as a tool for reconstructing social networks. Networks can be reconstructed from streaming data or data downloaded through the REST API. Because the REST API provides follower and friend information, it permits the reconstruction of all of a user's connections. A researcher interested in the complete social network of an individual therefore has to use the REST API.

Computationally analyzing text is a growing field in the social sciences (Grimmer and Stewart, 2013; Lucas *et al.*, 2015), and Twitter provides scholars with large corpora. The barriers to entry for appearing in a Twitter sample are substantially lower than for a news report or in Congress. People who are not likely to appear in those sources are therefore much more likely to appear on Twitter, casting light on swathes of previously unobservable behavior. While this outcome is true of the internet more broadly – barriers to entry are similarly low for joining most social networks, posting on web forums, or starting a blog – Twitter is unique in its combination of size and public communication. Elites who are likely to appear in traditional text sources usually have Twitter accounts (every Senator and 430 members of the House have official Twitter accounts, as do most news organizations), meaning Twitter records communication behavior from all strata of society. No other data source exists that is simultaneously comprehensive and accessible. For literature that applies natural language processing to Twitter, see Table 1.

It is also possible to map Twitter activity to specific places, allowing scholars to connect patterns on Twitter to offline events. Location information comes from two sources, accounts choosing to provide their GPS coordinates or self-reporting their location as part of their profile. Tweets with GPS coordinates, which represent 2–3% of all tweets (Leetaru *et al.*, 2013), provide the most precision in estimating location. Tweets with GPS coordinates are more prevalent in urban areas and among higher-income users, so the extent to which they are reliable depends on the research question (Malik *et al.*, 2015). See the Supplementary Materials for an analysis of which countries produce the most tweets with GPS coordinates, both in absolute and per capita terms. See Table 1 for examples of mapping Twitter to events.

## 1.3   A Note on Programming

Twitter data can be acquired, processed, and analyzed with many programming languages, including R and Python. R is the programming language most familiar to political scientists. An extension of S, a language developed at Bell Laboratories in the 1970s, R was designed by statisticians. While it can perform many general computation functions, its comparative advantage is in statistical analysis. When a new statistical procedure is developed, the first implementation is usually as an R package.

R can ingest Twitter data in three ways. streamR is a package that makes it easy to connect to R's streaming API and write the returned tweets to a .csv or JSON file (Barberá, 2013). twitteR is designed to work with the REST API, though the complexity of the REST API compared to the streaming one means the package is not as robust as streamR (Gentry, 2015). You could avoid these packages completely by using the RCurl package, which facilitates interaction with the HTTP endpoints that web services, including Twitter, use (Lang *et al.*, 2016). Using RCurl provides the most flexibility but requires more coding than using a package designed to work with Twitter.

Python is a general purpose language tracing its lineage to 1989 and is most famous for having easy to read code. Whereas R was created for data analysis and has been extended to other purposes, Python was created to work with computers and has been extended to data analysis. Transitioning from writing in R to writing in Python for the first time is much easier than transitioning from never having written code to writing in R.

The primary Python library for working with Twitter is twython (McGrath, 2015). (Tweepy is another Python library to access Twitter, but twython has a larger community and is more frequently updated). Unlike any R package, twython can work with Twitter's REST or streaming API and has built in exception handling. Python's pandas library provides data frames equivalent to R's as well as reshaping, merging, and aggregation capabilities spread across multiple R packages (McKinney, 2015); pandas is much faster than base R, though R's data.table package is as fast or even slightly faster than pandas (Dowle *et al.*, 2015). Python's statistical libraries are not as deep as R, though most parametric and non-parametric models are available through the statsmodels package (Seabold and Perktold,

2014). Libraries for Bayesian analysis are not as developed, though Stan has a Python interface. Python also has extensive libraries for natural language processing (Bird *et al.*, 2009) and machine learning (Mueller, 2015) if there are statistical domains in which Python strictly dominates R, it is these two.

Neither R nor Python strictly dominates the other. Python has more developed tools for scraping web pages, but Hadley Wickham's `rvest` package narrows this gap. Python is generally faster, but new R packages such as `data.table` erase that difference on some dimensions. R's syntax does not resemble that of other computer languages, but it is also easy to read and learn. The one area Python dominates R for data analysis is data storage: many more database products have Python libraries than R ones, though R has libraries for working with SQL, SQLLite, and MongoDB (a prominent NoSQL database). That said, most people are unlikely to need a database for their Twitter work. R dominates Python in developing aesthetically pleasing graphics, though a Python port of `ggplot` is being developed and Python's `matplotlib` library produces Matlib style graphics. If you already know R, learning Python may be worthwhile, but the costs and benefits require careful consideration since either language can most likely accomplish your programming task, and human time is the most scarce resource on any project. The more likely you are to work with large amounts of data or colleagues from outside the social sciences, the more beneficial Python knowledge becomes. If you know neither R nor Python, learn both.

## 2 Acquire Data from Twitter

There are three approaches to acquiring data: using Twitter's API, collaborating with those who have collected them, or purchasing them. This section details each in turn.

### 2.1 Acquire on Your Own

The first approach, and the one that is most likely to satisfy your research question, is to download the data yourself. Advantages of this approach include being able to define search terms, not relying on others for data, and, depending on how much data is involved, cost. Disadvantages include a steeper learning curve than purchasing or working with others, difficulty accessing historic data, and needing to maintain your own infrastructure. Sections 2.1.1 and 2.1.2 explain the two application programming interfaces (APIs) for acquiring data for free and what kinds of data are available from each. Though Twitter does not charge for using those interfaces, you still need hardware with which to store and analyze the data.

### 2.1.1   REST API

The REST API provides access to past tweets, user data, and social structure. Below, each paragraph explains the type of data the REST API provides. The italics at the beginning of the paragraph is the type of data; the paragraph then explains each type in detail.

*User's Tweets.* Twitter allows anyone to download an account's previous 3,200 tweets through the GET statuses/user_timeline endpoint. This endpoint accepts 180 requests per 15 minutes and returns up to 200 tweets per request. An account with 3,200 or more tweets will therefore require 16 requests. With each tweet, Twitter returns metadata on the tweet author, but that metadata reflect when the API request was made, not when the tweet was created. @Greptweet is a useful web interface on top of this endpoint.

*Specific Tweets.* More than 3,200 of a user's tweets can be downloaded if the identification number of each tweet is known. Since Twitter's Terms of Service prevent researchers from sharing more than 50,000 original tweets per day but allows an unlimited number of tweet IDs to be shared, a researcher who would like to replicate other work or use previous tweets in original research is therefore reliant on the goodwill of the original acquirer of the tweets and having the programmatic ability to download the tweets (see Freelon (2012) for an example of freely shared tweet IDs). Fortunately, Twitter's rate limits are generous for downloading tweets, and the code to do so is simple. You can download 18,000 tweets every 15 minutes (100 for each of 180 calls), equivalent to 1,728,000 per day. Downloading user information is subject to the same limits.

If you would like to download more than 1.7 million tweets per day, there are two options. The easiest approach – to split the list of IDs into small chunks and submit those chunks at the same time – will not work because Twitter only allows one connection per IP address. The two options for downloading tweets at a higher rate are therefore the two options to get around the IP limit. The first approach, which violates the spirit of Twitter's limit, is to route the requests through proxy servers. The second option is to use multiple computers. It is not difficult to launch multiple virtual instances using a hosting solution such as Amazon Web Services; the main drawback with a hosted solution is cost. Cost is substantially lessened if you use Amazon's t2.small instances and push the Twitter data to a local machine. Each t2.small instance costs $137–$180 annually, though you will also pay to transfer data. Otherwise, friends' computers or old machines are perfect for this sort of task; since downloading data is not computationally expensive, old computers are perfect for any Twitter task where rate limits force the task to take a long time.

*Search Tweets.* It is possible to query Twitter's GET search/tweets for old tweets matching certain parameters. This method is to be used cautiously, however, as Twitter returns only some tweets from the previous six to nine days and is not clear on how it chooses which to return. Only 100 tweets per request are returned, up to 180 requests per 15 minutes. To avoid receiving the same 100 results per request, pass the lowest tweet ID of the returned tweets to the max_id parameter in the subsequent call, and repeat this process as much as necessary. In addition to search terms, Twitter allows for filters based on language and latitude and longitude pairs; you can also specify for Twitter to return the most recent or most popular matching tweets, or a mix. One study has found that results from GET search/tweets do not match those from the random sample (González-Bailón *et al.*, 2012).

*User's Followers.* Reconstructing network connections is slightly more difficult. Two endpoints, GET followers/list and GET followers/ids, provide information about followers. The former provides fully hydrated user objects for each follower, up to 15 followers per 15 minutes. The latter provides only the identification number of followers, but it does so for 75,000 followers per 15 minutes; those numbers can then be fed to GET users/lookup, from which up to 18,000 completely hydrated user objects are returned every 15 minutes. GET followers/list therefore saves one step, but is slower than using GET followers/ids with GET users/lookup.

*User's Friends.* The same logic holds for retrieving who a user follows (that user's friends, in Twitter parlance). You connect to GET friends/ids instead of GET followers/ids, but those friend identification numbers are fed to GET users/lookup.

Twitter returns the follower and friend list in reverse chronological order but does not reveal when either connection is formed. Section 3.2.4 explains how to infer connection dates using the REST API.

### 2.1.2   Streaming API

This section details how to collect data in realtime via Twitter's streaming API.[1] There are two levels of access available, the 1% vs. 10% stream. Twitter removed free access to the 10% stream – variously called the garden hose or fire hose – in early 2011, and you now have to apply and pay for access. (Twitter does not disclose the price of connecting to the garden hose; anecdotally, it requires a large grant.) The 1% stream remains free and probably will forever, as it is the connection developers use to build Twitter-related

---

[1] The streaming API technically has three endpoints: GET statuses/sample, GET user, and GET site. Academics will only need to work with GET statuses/sample, so that is the connection assumed for the rest of this Element.

products. For documentation on the API, see Twitter developer guidelines. Because the streaming API returns all tweets matching filtering parameters so long as the total number of returned tweets is less than 1% of all tweets, these variations are different sets than a subset of tweets from the pure random sample matching those parameters.

*Random Sample.* By default, Twitter returns a random 1% sample of tweets as they are written. This sample comes out to about 5 million tweets and 12 gigabytes of raw data per day. Because each returned tweet object consists primarily of metadata, pre-processing or post-processing the tweets can reduce storage requirements without reducing the amount of useful data. Twitter does not disclose how it chooses the sample, leading to concern about the representativeness of the stream versus the complete Twitterverse. Comparisons of the stream to the complete Twitterverse find the stream does not differ in a meaningful manner (Morstatter *et al.*, 2013; Valkanas *et al.*, 2014).

You can also request Twitter filter the results from the streaming endpoint. If a filter is given, Twitter returns all tweets matching the request *up to 1% of all tweets.* For example, if you ask for every tweet with the keyword "LeBron" and tweets with that word constitute 1% of all tweets, Twitter will return every single tweet containing that word. This design is extremely advantageous for researchers, as it means the streaming sample can often become a streaming population. With filters, the streaming API can provide a researcher with every tweet of interest, though the researcher will have to know ahead of time what filters are of interest. To continue the keyword example, if the researcher connects to the stream without specifying "LeBron" only 1% of all tweets containing that word will be returned, 2 order of magnitude fewer tweets than requesting tweets specifically with "LeBron".

*Geographic Sample.* The streaming API can also return tweets from within a box defined by two coordinate pairs. The bounding boxes are not used in conjunction with other filters. For example, asking for tweets from San Francisco and tweets in Spanish will return all tweets from San Francisco (regardless of language) and all tweets in Spanish. Since 2–3% of tweets contain GPS coordinates (Leetaru *et al.*, 2013), passing the coordinate pairs [–180,90,180,90] – a box around the world – will return 33% to 50% of all tweet with GPS coordinates. Twitter accepts up to 25 bounding boxes per connection. The streaming API does not use a user's self-reported location.

*Specific Keywords.* Twitter will return tweets containing a user-supplied string, and multiple strings can be passed. This functionality can be used to search for specific hashtags, individual words, links (Twitter will search the expanded URL of a shortened link), retweets, or mentions of a user. Four hundred pieces of text can be passed per connection. Note that non-space separated languages, like Korean, Japanese, and Chinese, are not supported.

*Language Sample.* When connecting to the streaming API, you can request only tweets in a certain language. Twitter will then return all tweets in that language up to the 1% ceiling. Note that language cannot be the only parameter passed. To download tweets in a specific language, it is therefore best to pass generic keywords in that language, e.g. "this", "the", "is", and so on if you want a sample of tweets in English. The request will then return a random sample of the tweets in English that contain one of those words. Multiple languages can be requested simultaneously. Because Twitter does not filter for non-space separated languages, asking for tweets in those languages requires use of other parameters.

*Specific People.* You can submit specific user identification numbers to the streaming API and receive all tweets the users create, all tweets the users retweet, replies to tweets of the users, and retweets of the users' tweets. Five thousand people can be followed per connection. This feature is especially useful when the accounts to be studied are known. The best way to identify accounts is through lists, curated collections of accounts other users have created. For example, Twitter maintains the "US Senate" list, a list of the Twitter accounts for each Senator (every Senator has a Twitter account). A researcher could ask the REST API for the user identification number of each member of this list and then pass those numbers to the streaming API. Every tweet from every Senator would henceforth be downloaded by the user, assuming the 100 Senators never account for more than 1% of all tweets.

Except for the GPS bounding boxes, Twitter's documentation is not clear on how these parameters interact with each other. More likely than not, they are additive, e.g. following a specific user and asking for tweets in Spanish will probably return tweets in Spanish or tweets from that user.

### 2.1.3 Access Constraints and Replication

While Twitter's streaming and REST APIs are powerful, they have seven quirks to be aware of when writing code. These quirks render some kinds of analyses, especially those relying on the REST API, more difficult than they otherwise would be. They also raise the costs of replication, though full replication remains possible.

First, an overarching restriction is that Twitter imposes limits on how quickly you can retrieve data from the REST API. (The only restriction of the streaming API is that not every tweet is returned if the number of matching tweets exceeds 1% of the total volume of tweets.) Requests are counted in 15 minute windows, and most API endpoints allow 15 requests per window. Each request, however, may return multiple matches, and the number of matches returned is not constant across endpoints. For example, Twitter returns 5,000 followers per request, so 75,000 followers can be downloaded in one window. When asking Twitter for metadata about an account, 100 accounts per request and 180 requests per 15 minutes are allowed, allowing for metadata on 72,000 accounts every 15 minutes.

Download time is a step function. The amount of data returned in each request is small, so Twitter can return the results from 15 requests in a matter of seconds. A user with 75,000 followers therefore requires a few seconds to download the list of followers, but one with 75,001 requires just over 15 minutes.

If your code needs to query an endpoint more than the rate limit allows, the code must restrict itself, otherwise Twitter will sever the connection and reserves the right to ban the account from querying the APIs again. The rate limits make it very difficult to reconstruct complete social networks, an issue returned to in Section 3.2.4. Details on rate limits for specific endpoints are available at Twitter's developer website (https://developer.twit ter.com/en/docs/basics/rate-limits).

Second, Twitter only allows one connection per IP address to any part of its API. For example, downloading the 1% stream and a separate stream returning only tweets from the United States would require two separate IP addresses. Similarly, connecting to the stream while parsing accounts' followers requires two IP addresses. Without this restriction, the rate limits would be meaningless. Nonetheless, the ability to create virtual machines on demand, using a product such as Amazon Web Services, makes the IP address restriction less onerous than it otherwise would be.

Third, when asking for an account's previous tweets, the REST API returns only the 3,200 most recent tweets from an account. This restriction means that you will not obtain, for free, all the tweets from accounts which tweet often, such as celebrities, politicians, or media accounts. Because there is a positive relationship between tweet frequency and number of followers (Gonzalez-Bailon *et al.*, 2013), the limit means that a sample of users for whom all the tweets are available is a sample of less popular accounts. Moreover, the metadata of each tweet are not reflective of the tweet at the time it was authored. For example, a tweet from the streaming API will show how many followers the author has when the tweet is created, but that same tweet downloaded from the REST API will show the number of followers the account has at the time the old tweet was downloaded. This wrinkle means that tweets from the REST API are not equivalent to tweets from the stream API.

Fourth, while the REST API allows you to search historic tweets, the results are only from the previous seven to nine days and not exhaustive of those days. Twitter does not explain how it decides which tweets to return, so it should not be relied upon to reconstruct histories. Twitter only returns 100 results per request, up to 180 requests per 15 minutes.[2] A broad search with thousands of results may therefore take awhile to download and will not provide the population of tweets matching a search query. Searching directly at www.twitter.com returns all historic matches, but you cannot download those matches.

Fifth, Twitter only allows you to share 50,000 public tweets and/or accounts' metadata per day, and the sharing cannot be automated. For example, if a researcher uses more than 50,000 tweets for a paper and needs to share them, they cannot be made freely available. A system would need to be constructed to verify that an interested party is not downloading the data more than once per day, and the data cannot be pushed (sent automatically) to an interested party. Twitter does allow, however, the unlimited distribution of the numeric identification number of each tweet or user account. An interested party can then take these numbers to the REST API and download the full tweet and account information. But, as noted in the third limitation, the metadata from these tweets will differ from the metadata of the original tweets, if the original tweets were obtained from the streaming API.

Sixth, the streaming API occasionally disconnects. These disconnections are rare and random but can imperil research design if not caught quickly. At least three solutions are available. If your connection is designed to last indefinitely, that connection's code should generate an e-mail, or similar notification, whenever the connection is interrupted. Alternatively, you can intentionally disconnect from the streaming API and immediately reconnect at

---

[2] Technically, the number of requests depends on whether you are authenticated as a user or application. Since whether or not one form of authentication returns more results depends on the type of request and as most academics are not trying to build an application, the rate limits presented are for the user authentication.

preset intervals, such as every one to 24 hours. Any stoppage of the stream would therefore impact only that interval's data collection. (This strategy is what I employ in my data collection. I collect tweets in one hour intervals, using Unix systems' `cronjob` scheduling. My server launches a new script every hour, and that script only downloads tweets during those 60 minutes. Any disconnect in the previous hour will therefore cause me to lose no more than 60 minutes' data.) Third, you could implement a monitoring script that will restart the script whenever a disconnect notification is generated. This approach results in the least amount of data loss; the streaming API is very reliable, however, so the researcher should weigh the extra implementation time this check will require versus the hours of data it may save.

Seventh, when requesting specific users, best practice calls for using an identification number. When a user changes his or her username, Twitter does not update the user identification number corresponding to the original screen name. Asking either API for user information based on the screen name may therefore suffer from decay as users change their name, while asking by user identification number will not.

## 2.2   Collaborate

On April 14, 2010, Twitter and the Library of Congress announced the Twitter Research Access project, a collaboration to make every tweet ever published available to researchers (Stone, 2010). Scheduled for completion in 2013, the project still has not resulted in an available archive. Updates from the Library have been intermittent, though it is clear it has at least all tweets from 2006, when Twitter started, through the end of 2010. Disconcertingly, a report from the Library in 2013 suggested that the hardware necessary to enable fast searches of the archive are "cost-prohibitive and impractical for a public institution" (*Update on the Twitter Archive at the Library of Congress*, 2013). The most detailed report on the project and its current status is to be found in Zimmer (2015) and McGill (2016). The situation appears no closer to resolving itself.

@Greptweet hosts greptweet.com, a website that returns a user's 3,200 most recent tweets. This website is the most user friendly method to get a user's tweet history, but it suffers two main disadvantages. First, it only returns the tweet identification number, tweet timestamp, and tweet text; while you can retrieve the full tweet based on this information (see Section 2.1.1), it would be preferable to have the data without programming. Second, you can only get tweets for one user at a time, which is a much slower process than submitting requests through the API. greptweet.com is therefore best for retrieving data for a small group of people who do not tweet frequently.

TCAT allows an interested party to connect to Twitter's streaming API, follow users or keywords, and create network graphs through Gephi, all without any programming expertise (Ward, 2014). TCAT is best for identifying accounts that are influential in talking about a particular product. The service is no longer open to the public, though inquiries are accepted on an *ad hoc* basis (Groshek, 2015).

CrisisNet is part of Ushahidi, an open source digital platform that supports data-gathering from the internet and mobile phones, with a focus on the developing world and public sector implementations. CrisisNet ingests data from Ushahidi, Facebook, Twitter, Instagram, and ReliefWeb, processes the data into a standard form, and makes each post from each source available through an application programming interface. It is not a complete archive of content from the data sources it monitors; instead, it pays attention to specific accounts that CrisisNet users identify. Once an account is identified, its data from that point forward is part of CrisisNet. The platform is still a small operation and has the steepest learning curve of these tools.

Finally, many academics have already collected, or collect continuously, their own Twitter data, though Twitter's terms of service prevent the mass sharing of tweets. Collaborating with someone who already has Twitter data on a topic or timeframe of interest is often the quickest, most inexpensive method of acquiring tweets.

## 2.3  Purchase

If you are interested in tweets from the past, the most thorough approach is to purchase them from a vendor. (Section 2.1.1 describes how to download some old tweets for free.) Companies which provide access to old tweets pay a large, undisclosed licensing fee to Twitter, and their main customers are marketing and public relations firms. Since many companies provide this service, this section focuses on three of the most prominent.

The main vendor is Gnip; it was founded in 2008 and started licensing Twitter's data in 2010, and Twitter purchased the company outright in 2014. While Gnip's target market is businesses, anyone can purchase their old Twitter data using their Historical PowerTrack application programming interface (API). Gnip claims that prices start at $500, but a project will more likely spend upwards of $5,000 purchasing data. The price is a function of the number of tweets that will be returned and the timespan of the request, though the final price requires consultation with a sales representative. Gnip provides its own metadata as well, including expanded links, a Klout score, language detection, and enhanced geo-information. Though Gnip provides a programming interface, a one-time purchase is best handled through contacting a salesperson directly. Gnip has offered Data Grants, free downloads of tweets to winning applicants; its first, and so far only, competition, in 2014, saw 1,300 entrants compete for six grants.

DataSift is the second major reseller of archived tweets. They provide the same services as Gnip, provides a programming interface that uses their own syntax to filter historic data. (DataSift and Gnip also ingest other datasources such as Wikipedia, reddit, YouTube, and WordPress.) DataSift's historic data starts on January 1, 2010, whereas Gnip has every tweet since 2006. DataSift charges $1 per 5 hours of computation time, plus $0.10 per 1,000 tweets a query returns. To estimate the cost of a dataset, the researcher has to submit a query to DataSift's API. DataSift will return the estimated number of matching items, which, when divided by 10, will give the cost in dollars for the tweets themselves; the final cost will also include computation time. Two features distinguish DataSift from its competition. First, it accesses more services' data than other services. Second, DataSift has also published a Python library to access its API. An annual subscription costs $200, 000–$300,000.

The most cost-effective method to acquire historic tweets is through Texifter's Sifter tool. Texifter is a third-party vendor that interfaces with Gnip. The main advantage of Sifter is that it provides an online interface to Gnip's API so that a user can test a variety of search parameters. Sifter will then estimate the number of tweets the download would contain and provide a cost estimate. Sifter also appears to offer a lower price point than Gnip, though whether that is true or not is unclear since Gnip's pricing structure is opaque. Sifter then transfers the data to Texifter's DiscoverText tool, an online interface through which a coding team can search, filter, code, or analyze the returned tweets. The tweets can then be downloaded, though Twitter's terms of service require that Sifter only allow 50,000 tweets per day to be downloaded, regardless of how many match a user's query.

## 3  Process Data

### 3.1  Getting Started

This section takes the reader through creating a Twitter account and creating an application with that account. The application is what will connect to Twitter's APIs, and an account can own multiple applications.

Section 3.1.1 explains how to create an account, and Section 3.1.2 shows how to use that account to obtain the credentials you will need to access Twitter's API. Section 3.2 provides Python and R scripts to download a user's tweets, download specific tweets by their identification number, search for tweets, download an account's followers, and download an account's friends (the accounts the account follows). Section 3.3 provides Python and R scripts to download a 1% random sample of the Twitter stream as well as request tweets from the stream that match language, geographic, account, or keyword parameters. The sections show the key line or lines that download the data and provide links to the full script. Each script is designed to run manually, so there is redundancy in the first lines of each.

### 3.1.1   Create an Account

1. Load Twitter (www.twitter.com) in your internet browser.[3]
2. On the right side of the browser window, you will see a box that says "New to Twitter? Sign Up", as Image 1 shows. Fill that box with your name, contact e-mail address, and a password.

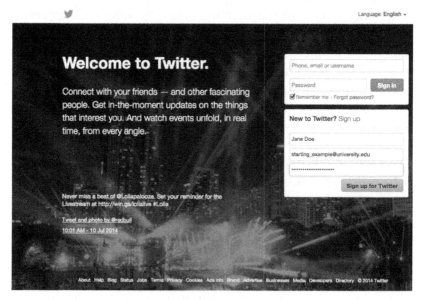

**Image 1.**

---

[3] These steps are current as of May 2016.

3. After entering your name, contact e-mail address, and a password, click the yellow button that says "Sign Up for Twitter".

4. The website will load a new screen (Image 2). Enter your name, contact e-mail address, and password again. Add your desired username, which is what your primary name will be on Twitter. Uncheck the boxes about staying signed in and tailoring Twitter, if you desire.

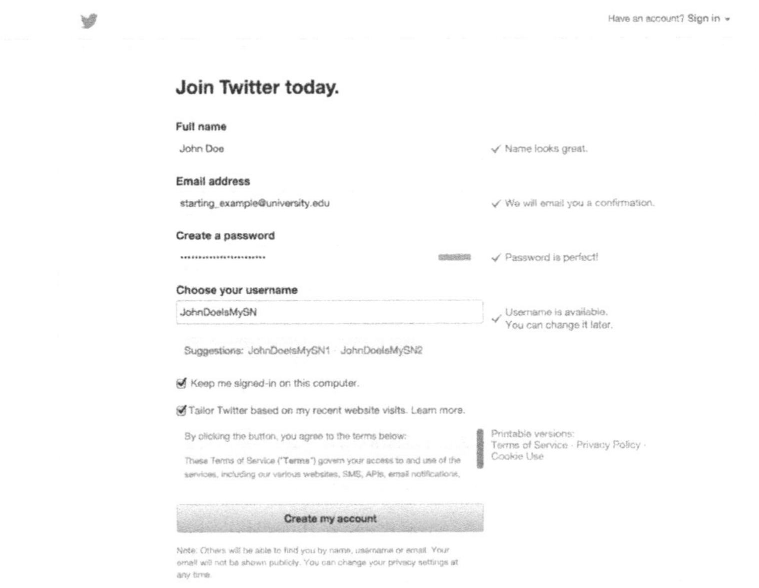

**Image 2.**

5. Click the yellow "Create my account" button after completing the previous step.

6. In the screen that loads after clicking the "Create my account" button, follow steps 1–5. These steps provide Twitter with more information about yourself. Since this account will be for research purposes, it is not important to answer these. Note that there is a small phrase, "Skip this step", at the bottom right

of your screen; clicking those words will allow you to progress to the next page.

7. After completing those steps, you will arrive on your Twitter homepage. You will see a banner notifying you about a confirmation e-mail and giving you options to resend the e-mail, change your e-mail address, or get help (the "learn more" text). See Image 3.

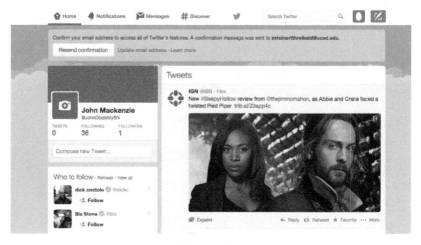

**Image 3.**

8. Check your e-mail using the e-mail address you gave Twitter. You will have an e-mail with a blue "Confirm now" button. Click that button. If you do not see this e-mail after a few minutes, check your Spam folder.

9. Clicking the "Confirm now" button will take you to the Twitter homepage for your account, as shown in Image 4. It is worth following some accounts and sending a couple of tweets immediately so Twitter does not delete your account for inactivity.

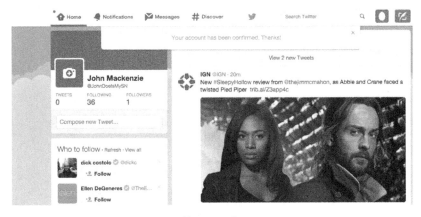

**Image 4.**

### 3.1.2 Register an Application

Before you can request data from Twitter, you will have to prove to Twitter that you actually have an account. Proving is accomplished through the OAuth authentication standard. This section will show you how to authenticate yourself with Twitter.

1. Use your internet browser to load www.dev.twitter.com. If you are not still logged in from Step 1, you will see a screen similar to Image 5. Twitter changes their background image often, so do not worry if your webpage does not look exactly like this.

**Image 5.**

2. Move your mouse to "Developers." A menu will drop down. Click on "Documentation". See Image 6.

**Image 6.**

3. A new page will load after clicking "Documentation". On the left navigation bar of that new page, click "Manage My Apps".
4. Twitter will tell you that you do not have any applications yet, as Image 7 shows. Click "Create New App".

**Image 7.**

5. The next screen, shown in Image 8, is where you create your application, which is what you will use to access Twitter's API. Fill in the fields with whatever words you want, though it is best that the name and description correlate with the purpose of the application. The website field can be any website, unrelated to you or not. Once the fields are completed, check the "Yes, I agree" box for the Developer Rules of the Road[4] and click the "Create your Twitter application" button.

---

[4] You should also read the rules of the road. They are short and explain the limits to sharing tweets.

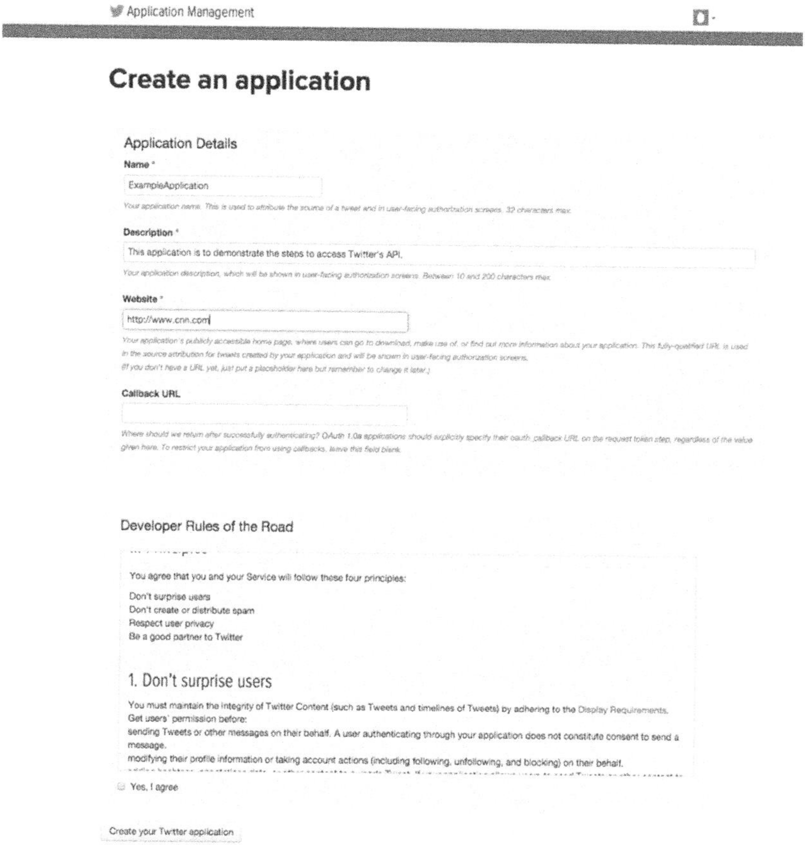

**Image 8.**

6. After creating your application, you will find yourself at the main page for your application and see four navigation tabs – "Details", "Settings", "Keys and Access Tokens", and "Permissions". Click on "Keys and Access Tokens".

7. After clicking on "Keys and Access Tokens", your screen should look like Image 9, with your application's name in large, bold font. Note that the application name has changed from "ExampleApplicationNeophytes" to "ExampleApplication" because the latter was taken.

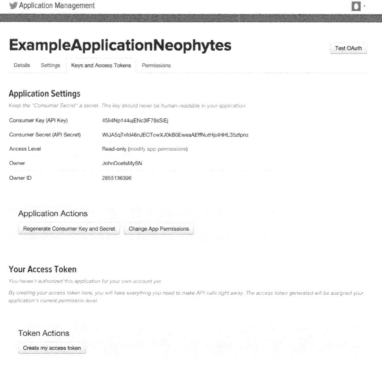

**Image 9.**

8. Copy and paste the "Consumer Key (API Key)" and "Consumer Secret (API Secret)" fields somewhere you can easily retrieve them, such as in a text document. These will be necessary soon. *The method of connecting to the streaming API through R does not require the next steps; if you are using R, skip to "Use R to Verify Your Identity". Libraries in other languages will accept the two items created in the next steps or let you replicate the steps R requires.*

9. At the bottom of the screen, click the "Create my access token" button.

10. Once you click the "Create my access token" button, the screen will refresh, with more information displayed under the "Your Access Token" section. If there is no information, wait a few minutes and click the "Refresh" blue text at the top of the screen. Your screen should look like Image 10:

**Image 10.**

11. Copy and paste the "Access Token" and "Access Token Secret"
    fields somewhere you can easily retrieve them, such as in a text
    document. You will also need these shortly.

## 3.2   Using the REST API

R's `twitteR` package is designed to work with the REST API and is
used in the following examples. Its documentation is not user
friendly, but there are many examples online of how to use it to

accomplish common Twitter tasks. An alternative option is to access the API directly through `PycURL` or `RCurl`; those libraries use Python and R to work with `curl` and `libcurl`, lower level tools to transfer files via the internet. Working directly with the API entails submitting requests as long URLs and provides the most flexibility to the researcher. Since that approach has a steeper learning curve than working with a library designed for Twitter, it will not be presented here.

### 3.2.1   User's 3,200 Tweets

The full R script to download a user's tweets is here (www .cambridge.org/download_file/949248). The key line is this:

```
1 tweets <- userTimeline(user, n = 3200, includeRts = TRUE)
  # n = 3200 ensures all tweets will be downloaded; Twitter
  does not return more than 3200 tweets.
```

tweets is a list, and the twListToDF() function converts that list to a data frame. The script also shows how to save the tweet identification numbers to a text file, a necessary step for others to replicate your work.

The full Python script to download a user's tweets is here (www .cambridge.org/download_file/949245). The script defines a function to retrieve a user's tweets using either the screen name or identification number, and it can be easily extended to handle multiple users at once. It also contains a function to save the tweets to a file. The key lines are:

```
1 temp = connection.get_user_timeline(screen_name=-
    screen_name, count=200, max_id=maxID - 1)
2
3 tweets = getUserTweets(screen_name='ZacharyST')
4 saveTweets(tweets, filename='<insert_your_name_here')
```

### 3.2.2 Tweets by ID

You can download specific tweets if the tweet identification number is known. This feature is useful if you want to replicate other Twitter studies: Twitter does not allow you to share more than 50,000 raw tweets per day, but you can share an unlimited number of tweet identification numbers. For tweet identification numbers, Twitter returns 6,000 tweets per 15 minutes, or 576,000 per day. For an example of a researcher sharing tweets, see Freelon (2012).

The full R script to download specific tweets is here (www .cambridge.org/download_file/949242). The key lines are:

```
1  # Load one tweet
2  tweet <- showStatus(tweet_IDs$ID [1])
3
4  # Multiple tweets require more work
5  chunkedTweets <- split(tweet_IDs$ID, ceiling(seq_along
      (tweet_IDs$ID)/ submissionsPerRequest)) # ceiling
      (seq_along(tweet_ IDs$ID)/ submissionsPerRequest)
      generates a list of repeating numbers for split () to
      split. split then creates a list where each entry is as
      long as submissionsPerRequest (100 in this example).
6
7  tweets <- NULL # Empty object that tweets will feed into
8
9  # Download tweets
10 for(i in 1:length(chunkedTweets)){
11    print (paste ( 'On cycle ', i, 'of tweets ', sep=' '))
      # Status tracker
12    # Sys. sleep (delay) # How many seconds to pause so that do
      not trip rate limit. Commented out in this loop because
      downloading 3,200 tweets will never exceed the rate
      limit. (60 requests * 100 tweets per request) > 3200
      tweets
13    temp <- twListToDF(lookup_statuses(ids = chunkedTweets
      [[i]]))
14    tweets <- rbind(tweets, temp)
15 }
```

The full Python script to download specific tweets is here (www .cambridge.org/download_file/949239). The key lines are:

```
1  # Download tweets
2  for chunk in chunkedTweets:
3      print('On new chunk')
4      temp = connection.lookup_status(id=chunk) # Notice that
           this is lookup_status and not show_status
5      tweets.extend([item for item in temp])
```

### 3.2.3  Search Tweets

Twitter's REST API also allows you to search for recent tweets by calling the GET search/tweets endpoint. The parameters you can pass are quite similar to the parameters the streaming API accepts, but the search function only returns tweets from the previous six to nine days. (Twitter's documentation variously states the previous seven days or the previous six to nine days.) If you are interested in tweets related to an unexpected event, it is easier to connect to the streaming API and pass the same parameters you would to GET search/tweets. GET search/tweets is therefore best used to observe the world in the period just before an unexpected event happens, not to watch the world in real time.

The search functionality treats geolocation different from the streaming API. In the streaming API, a bounding box is passed, and Twitter returns tweets with GPS coordinates from within that box. When searching for tweets, you supply a point and a radius around that point (in miles or kilometers), and Twitter returns tweets from within that circle. In addition, the streaming API only returns tweets with GPS coordinates, whereas the search function will return matches based on a user's self-reported location. For example, if you are a user who says they are from New York City, New York and tweets without GPS coordinates, you will have your tweet returned via the REST API search but not through the streaming API.

While this approach would appear to advantage the search endpoint, that endpoint's location functionality is circumspect. The example in this section's script (www.cambridge.org/download_file/949224) asks for tweets within five miles of New York

City that contain the acronym "NBA". None of the tweets contains GPS coordinates, and the self-reported location of many of the users is unmistakably not within five miles of the city. For example, one user is from "Philly", another from "ALABAMA", and another from "Watching a Game Somewhere." The original tweets can be found at this link (www.cambridge.org/download_file/949236).

The full R script to search for tweets matching specific criteria is here (www.cambridge.org/download_file/949224). The key lines are:

```
1 # How many tweets to return per query
2 size <- 1000 # Modify as needed
3
4 # One word
5 nba_tweets <- searchTwitter('nba', n = size) # Also returns
    hashtags, and Twitter is not case sensitive.
6 nba_tweets <- twListToDF(nba_tweets) # Could shorten
    these two lines to nba_tweets <- twListToDF
    (searchTwitter('nba', n = size))
```

The full Python script that does the same is here (www .cambridge.org/download_file/949221). The key lines are:

```
1 # Connect
2 connection = twy.Twython(APP_KEY, APP_SECRET,
    OAUTH_TOKEN, OAUTH_TOKEN_SECRET)
3
4 # How many tweets to return per query
5 size = 100 # Modify as needed, maximum is 100
6
7 # One word
8 nba_tweets = connection.search(q='nba', count=size)
    # Also returns hashtags, and Twitter is not case
    sensitive.
```

Both scripts include examples for searching for multiple terms, excluding a tweet if it contains a term, searching for user mentions, returning tweets with images, returning tweets with links, filtering by language, and filtering by geolocation. They also contain a simple example of using the search functionality to build a dataset in real time.

### 3.2.4  Followers

The full R script to download a user's followers is here (www .cambridge.org/download_file/949218). The key lines are:

```
1 account <- getUser ( 'ZacharyST' )
2 total_followers <- account$followersCount
3 account_followers <- twListToDF (account$getFollowers
    (n = total_followers) # Create data frame from list of
    followers of account
```

The R script provides code for getting the followers of one account but not of multiple accounts. The simplest approach to automating the followers download for multiple accounts is to generate a function that applies lines 30–77 of the script to each account in the list of accounts whose followers you want. A faster approach, however, is to download the follower identification numbers of all followers of all accounts and deduplicate before downloading the complete user profile. That exercise is left to the reader.

The full Python script to download a user's followers is here (www.cambridge.org/download_file/949215). The key lines are:

```
1 ##### Get followers for a very popular account
2 account = connection.lookup_user(screen_name=
    ['BarackObama'])
3 account_followers = account[0]['followers_count']
4
5 get_followers(user='BarackObama', cursor=-1, total_-
    followers=account_followers)
6
7 ###### Hydrate followers list. Below function just get
    list of Twitter IDs.
8 ids = openIDs(user='BarackObama')
9
```

```
10 total = len(ids)
11 i = 0
12 while i < total:
13     print(("On follower \%d") \% i)
14     j = i + 100
15     hydrateFollowers(user='BarackObama', IDs=ids,
         start=i, end=j)
16     i += 100
17     pct_done = (j / total) * 100
18     print(("Finished \%f10 percent") \% pct_done)
```

As with the R script, this script can easily be extended to retrieve followers for multiple users. That exercise is left to the reader.

The scripts show how to heed rate limits when an account has many followers. Downloading followers from an account with more than 5,000 followers will exceed the rate limits, unless the script accounts for those limits.

### 3.2.5  Following

The full R script to download a user's friends is here (www .cambridge.org/download_file/949212). The key lines are:

```
1 account <- getUser('ZacharyST')
2 total_friends <- account$friendsCount
3 account_friends <- twListToDF(account$getFriends
    (n = total_friends)) # Create data frame from list of
    friends of account
```

The full Python script to download a user's friends is here (www .cambridge.org/download_file/949209). The key lines are:

```
1 ##### Get friends for a very popular account
2 account = connection.lookup_user(screen_name=
    ['BarackObama'])
3 account_friends = account[0]['friends_count']
4
5 get_friends(user='BarackObama', cursor=-1, total_-
    friends=account_friends)
6
```

```
 7
 8
 9 ###### Hydrate friends list. Below function just get list
   of Twitter IDs.
10 ids = openIDs(user='BarackObama')
11
12 total = len(ids)
13 i = 0
14 while i < total:
15    print(("On friend \%d") \% i)
16    j = i + 100
17    hydrateFriends(user='BarackObama', IDs=ids, start=i,
        end=j)
18    i += 100
19    pct_done = (j / total) * 100
20    print(("Finished \%f10 percent") \% pct_done)
```

## 3.3   Using the Streaming API

This section provides scripts for how to connect to Twitter's streaming API and pass various parameters to it. Note that each R script uses your consumer key and consumer secret strings to generate an OAuth access token, but you only have to do that once. For example, if at *t*=0 you generate an access token, at all future points you can load that access token instead of generating a new one. The Python scripts do not create an access token, requiring you to submit your key and secret strings each time.

In each R script, the argument timeout = 30 is used, which tells streamR to download tweets for 30 seconds. This parameter should be modified for your needs; 0 means maintain the connection indefinitely, and the maximum value is 10800 (3 hours). In my connections, I maintain the connection for one hour (timeout = 3600) and use a service called cron to start the script every hour. (cron is a Unix utility already installed on OS X and most distribution of Linux. See this page for information on a cron equivalent in Windows. Here is a tutorial on cron jobs, and here are the Google results for "cron tutorial".) This way, any break in the stream will cause you to miss no more than 60 minutes of data. This approach requires file names to change dynamically, and this script shows how to create a function to do that (www.cambridge.org/down load_file/949203).

Scripts can include the time the connection was created in the file name. This naming convention makes it very easy to find tweets within a specific timeframe later. Finally, if you use cron to run the script, you will need to add a "shebang", a first line which tells the operating system which program to use to execute the following lines.

The longer you maintain a connection, the more data you will miss if the connection is interrupted; for example, making a connection every three hours will lose two hours of data if the connection is severed after one hour. On the other hand, making a connection last for only one minute minimizes the effect of connection interruptions but increases the workload on your computer. If you write one file per connection, you will have 60 times more files than writing one every hour. It is not necessarily bad to have so many files, but it can slow down later retrieval of data. You should absolutely not maintain an indefinite connection because the resulting file will be too large to load into RAM, significantly slowing down, and possibly crashing, your computer.

In each Python script, timeout functionality is handled by asking the script to compare the current time to the time when the script started. If that time is greater than a user-defined limit, the script stops. As with R, the following script (www.cambridge.org/down load_file/949200) collects tweets for 60 minutes, under the assumption that it is launched as a cron job every hour.

The below code extract shows the base code the Python scripts use. In the following subsections, only the modified streamConnect function is shown.

```
1  # Import libraries
2  import twython as twy
3  import json
4  import datetime as dt
5
```

```
 6 # Key, secret, token, token_secret for one of my developer
      accounts.
 7 # Update with your own strings as necessary
 8 APP_KEY = 'yourConsumerKey'
 9 APP_SECRET = 'yourConsumerSecret'
10 OAUTH_TOKEN = 'yourAccessToken'
11 OAUTH_TOKEN_SECRET = 'yourAccessTokenSecret'
12
13 # Make class
14 class MyStreamer(twy.TwythonStreamer):
15    fileDirectory = '/path/to/directory/to/save/to/' # Any
         result from this class will save to this directory
16
17    stop_time = dt.datetime.now() + dt.timedelta(min-
         utes=60) # Connect to Twitter for 60 minutes. Comment
         out if do not want it timed.
18
19    def on_success(self, data):
20        if dt.datetime.now() > self.stop_time: # Once min-
             utes=60 have passed, stop. Comment out these 2
             lines if do not want timed connection.
21          raise Exception('Time_expired')
22
23        fileName = self.fileDirectory + 'Tweets_' + dt.date-
             time.now().strftime("\%Y_\%m_\%d_\%H") + '.
             txt' # File name includes date out to hour.
24        open(fileName, 'a').write(json.dumps(data) +
             '\n') # Append tweet to the file
25        # Because the file name includes the hour, a new file is
             created automatically every hour.
26
27    def on_error(self, status_code, data):
28        fileName = self.fileDirectory + dt.datetime.now().
             strftime("\%Y_\%m_\%d_\%H") + '_Errors.txt'
29        open(fileName, 'a').write(json.dumps(data) + '\n')
30
31
32 # Make function. Tracks key words.
33 def streamConnect(APP_KEY, APP_SECRET, OAUTH_TOKEN,
      OAUTH_TOKEN_SECRET):
34    stream = MyStreamer(APP_KEY, APP_SECRET, OAUTH_TOKEN,
         OAUTH_TOKEN_SECRET)
35    stream.statuses.sample()
36
```

```
37 # Execute
38 streamConnect(APP_KEY, APP_SECRET, OAUTH_TOKEN,
     OAUTH_TOKEN_SECRET)
```

### 3.3.1   Random Sample

The full R script to download the 1% sample is provided at this link (www.cambridge.org/download_file/949197). The key line is this:

```
1 sampleStream(file.name = 'raw_tweets.txt', oauth =
     my_oauth, timeout = 30) # This saves tweets in their raw
     form as /path/to/your/working/directory/raw_tweets.
     txt. Closes after 30 seconds.
```

The full Python script to download the 1% sample is provided at this link (www.cambridge.org/download_file/949194). It is the same as the extract provided at the beginning of Section 3.3.

### 3.3.2   Language Sample

The full R script to download a language sample is provided at this link (www.cambridge.org/download_file/949191). The key line is this:

```
1 filterStream(file.name='raw_tweets_language.txt', time-
     out = 30, track = 'a, an, the, and, but, is, this, that',
     oauth = my_oauth, language = 'en') # Use filler words to
     capture a large amount of tweets.
```

The full Python script to download a language sample is provided at this link (www.cambridge.org/download_file/949188). The key lines are:

```
1 # Make function
2 def streamConnect(APP_KEY, APP_SECRET, OAUTH_TOKEN,
     OAUTH_TOKEN_SECRET):
3    stream = MyStreamer(APP_KEY, APP_SECRET,
       OAUTH_TOKEN, OAUTH_TOKEN_SECRET)
```

```
4   stream.statuses.sample(track=['a, an, the, and, but,
        is, this, that, on, in, up, to'], language=['en'])
```

Note the use of specific keywords in the 'track' argument. Twitter will not return a purely random sample of tweets in a language. Instead, it will use language as a secondary filter to tweets that match other parameters. It is therefore a good idea to use a large number of generic words. The downloaded tweets are thus a random sample of the tweets containing at least one tracked keyword, and a sufficiently long list of keywords should approximate a random sample of the population of tweets in that language.

### 3.3.3   Geographic Sample

The full R script to download a sample of tweets with GPS coordinates is provided at this link (www.cambridge.org/download_file/ 949185). The key line is this:

```
1 filterStream(file.name = 'tweets_GPS.txt', timeout = 30,
      oauth = my_oauth, location = c(-180,-90,180,90))
```

The full Python script to download a sample of tweets with GPS coordinates is provided at this link (www.cambridge.org/down load_file/949182). The key lines are:

```
1 # Make function
2 def streamConnect(APP_KEY, APP_SECRET, OAUTH_TOKEN,
      OAUTH_TOKEN_SECRET):
3     stream = MyStreamer(APP_KEY, APP_SECRET,
          OAUTH_TOKEN, OAUTH_TOKEN_SECRET)
4     stream.statuses.filter(locations=[-180, -90, 180, 90])
```

Either script downloads tweets with a GPS coordinate from anywhere in the world. Because 2–3% of tweets have GPS coordinates, asking for any tweet with a GPS coordinate will generate a sample containing $\frac{1}{3} - \frac{1}{2}$ of all tweets with GPS coordinates. Narrowing the bounding box is therefore likely to generate a dataset that is the population of tweets from a specific locale; for example, a bounding box surrounding Iceland will provide the population of geolocated tweets from there. The R script gives examples for downloading any tweet with GPS coordinates, any tweet outside of the United States, and tweets from multiple locations. The Python script shows only a global bounding box, but the coordinates from the R script for the other bounding boxes also work in the Python script.

### 3.3.4 Specific Text

The full R script to stream tweets containing certain keywords is provided at this link (www.cambridge.org/download_file/949179). The key line is this:

```
1 filterStream(file.name='tweets_keywords.txt', timeout =
    30, track='LeBron James, Steph Curry, NBA, basketball,
    Warriors, GSW, Cavaliers, espn com', oauth = my_oauth)
```

The full Python script to stream tweets containing certain keywords is provided at this link (www.cambridge.org/download_file/949176). The key lines are:

```
1 def streamConnect(APP_KEY, APP_SECRET, OAUTH_TOKEN,
    OAUTH_TOKEN_SECRET):
2     stream = MyStreamer(APP_KEY, APP_SECRET,
        OAUTH_TOKEN, OAUTH_TOKEN_SECRET)
3     stream.statuses.filter(track=['LeBron James,
        Steph Curry, NBA, basketball, Warriors, GSW,
        Cavaliers, espn com'])
```

Each script downloads tweets about basketball, with an emphasis on the 2016 NBA Finals, one of the greatest Finals series of all time. Twitter treats multiple word phrases as having a Boolean AND, so a phrase like "LeBron James" will return tweets such as "LeBron James is ready for the game" and "My brother James likes

LeBron"; results are not case sensitive, so "lebron james is ready for the game" matches as well. "espn com" is the recommended way to download any tweet from the espn.com domain. Finally, note there are no spaces after the commas; Twitter will treat those as characters to match, so "Steph Curry is ready for the game" would not match if the term passed is ". . ., Steph Curry"

### 3.3.5    Specific people

The full R script to download tweets in real time from specific accounts is provided at this link (www.cambridge.org/download_ file/949179). The key line is this:

```
1 filterStream(file.name='tweets_accounts.txt', timeout =
     30, oauth = my_oauth, follow = '813286,1536791610')
     # @BarackObama, @POTUS
```

The full Python script to download tweets in real time from specific accounts is provided at this link (www.cambridge.org /download_file/949176). The key lines are:

```
1 # Make function
2 def streamConnect(APP_KEY, APP_SECRET, OAUTH_TOKEN,
     OAUTH_TOKEN_SECRET):
3     stream = MyStreamer(APP_KEY, APP_SECRET,
         OAUTH_TOKEN,OAUTH_TOKEN_SECRET)
4     stream.statuses.filter(follow=
         ['813286,1536791610'])
```

The streaming API requires users' identification number be used, not their screen name. The identification number can be downloaded via the REST API or from this website. Accounts can change their screen name, but their identification number is permanent.

## 3.4 Converting to Local Time

All tweets are delivered with a `created_at` field for the date and time the tweet was created. Twitter sets this information, however, to Greenwich Mean Time, which can pose a problem for analyses incorporating Twitter into offline events. To ensure the `created_at` field aligns with the local time of the author of the tweet, not the time in Great Britain, the researcher must undertake a few additional steps.

If the tweet does not contain GPS coordinates, it most likely contains a field in the user field called `utc_offset`. ("Most likely" because this field only exists if a user has identified his or her timezone in his or her profile; Twitter does not guess the timezone. In my experience, 65% of users do so.) This field gives the time, in seconds, by which the user's self-identified timezone differs from Greenwich Mean Time. The researcher adds this value to `created_at` to estimate the local time an account created a tweet. This new time is an estimate because it is possible the tweet author created the tweet in a different timezone than that indicated in the profile.

If the tweet contains GPS coordinates, the local time it was created is known with certainty. With precise location information, you can identify the timezone of the tweet and adjust accordingly.

The full Python script to adjust `created_at` to local time is here (www.cambridge.org/download_file/949173). The key lines are:

```
1 ### If tweet contains GPS coordinates
2 # Get GPS pair, SW corner of bounding box from Twitter
3 longitude = tweet['place']['bounding_box']['coordi-
     nates'][0][0][0]
4 latitude = tweet['place']['bounding_box']['coordi-
     nates'][0][0][1]
5
6 # Get timezones
7 tf = TimezoneFinder()
8 zone = tf.timezone_at(lng=longitude, lat=latitude)
     # Gives string of name of timezone
9 timezone = pytz.timezone(zone) # Convert string to pytz
```

```
        format
10
11 # Make local time
12 utc_time = dt.datetime.strptime(tweet['created_at'],
       '%a_\%b_\%d_\%H:\%M:\%S_ +0000_\%Y').replace(tzinfo=-
       pytz.UTC) # Convert tweet timestamp to datetime object
13 local_time = utc_time.replace(tzinfo=pytz.utc).
       astimezone(timezone) # Get local time as datetime object
14
15 ### If tweets do not contain GPS coordinates
16 # Correct for user timezone
17 utc_time = dt.datetime.strptime(tweet['created_at'],
       '%a_\%b_\%d_\%H:\%M:\%S_ +0000_\%Y')
18 local_time = utc_time + dt.timedelta(seconds=tweet
       ['user']['utc_offset']) # Subtract hours based on
       timezone from profile
```

## 3.5 Improving Location

When a tweet contains GPS coordinates, Twitter adds the location name from where the tweet originated. Most of the time – approximately 85% in my experience – this location name is the city and is correct. The rest of the time, however, the location information is instead a "point of interest" (Twitter's phrase, referring to prominent landmarks or locations), city neighborhood, or administrative region (state, in the United States). For example, a point of interest could be "888 Vietnamese Restaurant", a location probably too precise for most analysts; reverse geocoding reveals that this restaurant is in Austin, Texas. The reverse problem also exists: Twitter resolves many small towns to the state level, meaning an analyst can improve the precision of these points with reverse geocoding; for example, it commonly codes Druid Hills, North Carolina as only North Carolina and Vandenberg Air Force Base as California. Finally, Twitter can provide neighborhood names such as Boston's Financial District or SoMa (South of Market) in San Francisco; a reverse geocoder will reveal to which city those neighborhoods belong.

The key is to feed the tweet's GPS coordinates to a reverse geocoding package. I prefer Python's `reverse_geocoder` package. The code provided at this link (www.cambridge.org/down load_file/949170) shows how to do that. If Twitter indicates the place is a city, it keeps the city name Twitter assigns. If Twitter calls the place a "poi", "neighborhood", or "admin", it feeds the tweet's GPS coordinate to the `reverse_geocoder` package. The code preserves the place name Twitter assigns so that the point of interest or neighborhood can be preserved for future reference; it also adds county and state names. The key lines are:

```
1  if(tweet['place']['place_type'] == 'city'):
2  tweet['city'] = tweet['place']['name']
3
4  if(tweet['place']['place_type'] != 'city'): # If the pla-
      ce_type is admin, neighborhood, or poi
5      # Other processing not shown here but that is in the
      script
6      tweet['reversegeocode_results'] = rg.search(tweet
      ['place.bounding_box.SWcorner_rg']) # Perform
      reverse geocode
7      tweet['city'] = [item['name'] for item in tweet
      ['reversegeocode_results']]
```

## 3.6 Storing Tweets

Approximately 5 million tweets per day are available to researchers via the streaming API. Uncompressed, these tweets require approximately 12 gigabytes per day. A researcher therefore needs the capacity to store these tweets and later access them quickly. Because of the size of these data and the need to maintain a continuous connection to the streaming API, it is a good idea to have a dedicated computer with as much RAM as possible.

The easiest way to reduce the storage space required is to compress (zip) the files. A common compression protocol is `gzip`, and it is freely available in Unix operating systems. While the amount of space saved will vary by the kind of file, my experience is that gzipped tweets require approximately 16% of the space of unzipped ones.

To make the files even smaller, you can remove certain fields from each tweet. This subsetting can be done as the tweet arrives or once it is stored in a file. This procedure is useful because many fields in a tweet, such as the background image URL, may not be necessary depending on the project. An example of a script that reads downloaded tweets, keeps certain fields, and saves a new file is provided here (www.cambridge.org/download_file/949167). After removing fields in which I am not interested and compressing the file, my tweets are 6.67% of their original size (the final reduction will depend on which fields and compression you use).

I do not recommend, however, removing tweet fields, for three reasons. First, it throws away data, which is never a good idea. Second, it removes the flexibility of JSON formatting, which means it is brittle to changes in tweet metadata Twitter may makes. For example, that script does not extract image or video URLs that are now provided. Any time Twitter adds new fields to a tweet, the script will require updating. When downloading raw JSON files, you do not have to worry about changes in how the tweet is formatted. Third, tools exist to automatically convert JSON to dataframe formats. Python's `pandas` library will do this, as will the `csvkit` toolkit. The script is thus redundant with more robust tools.

The two broad approaches to storing tweets are as flat files or in a database. "Flat file" is data in raw text form; it can be read by any text editing program, like a normal file. A .csv file is an example of a flat file.

A database is an indexed collection of files; searches for items in the files are queries of the index, increasing the speed of queries and potentially decreasing the memory load on a computer. Databases can only be explored via specialized programs or scripts, i.e. the R command `read.csv` cannot read a database.

Within the database world are two flavors: structured and semi-structured databases. Structured data are data where each datum has the same variables. For example, all bills in a database of legislation will have values for date, sponsor, number of words, and so on. Structured data resemble the spreadsheets that most people are comfortable working with. Databases which store these data are known as SQL databases after the main language for querying them, Structured Query Language (SQL). Many kinds of data, especially from social media, do not have the same variables for each datum. For example, a tweet downloaded from Twitter will list the hashtags, links, and user mentions it contains if the tweet text has any; if none exists, an empty list is returned. Twitter will also identify any stock symbols in a tweet as long as they are proceeded by a dollar sign and are uppercase. A tweet with zero hashtags therefore looks different than one with one, and one with one looks different than one with two.

While a researcher can create a structured database that accounts for this eventuality, it is unwise to do so. First, it is important to define how many columns to create for the variable that may or may not exist. Returning to the hashtag example, a tweet could contain up to 47 hashtags.[5] Constructing the database requires similar calculations for user mentions, stock symbols, and links. You can create a SQL database with as many columns as possible variables, but doing so leads to a much larger database than is required. Second, Twitter could decide to change the actual data a tweet contains. For example, in April 2013, Twitter added annotation to tweets if they contained stock symbols. Attempting to load a tweet with a stock symbol would crash the database script, preventing subsequent tweets without stock symbols from entering the database. Your script can be structured to avoid this problem, but then you would miss the data on stock symbols. Structured databases are not ideal for semi-structured data.

Semi-structured databases, commonly called NoSQL databases, are designed designed to work with data whose representation can

---

[5] The smallest hashtag is two characters, e.g. "#a", and hashtags will have a space character separating them, except for the final hashtag. Solving $2x + x - 1 \leq 140$, $x = 47$.

vary for each datum. There is not a dominant query language for semi-structured data; the two most common are Cassandra and MongoDB. Cassandra started at Facebook but is now an open source project, and it did not originally handle JSON objects (tweets are delivered as JSON objects). MongoDB is the preferred database for JSON objects and is therefore the one most commonly used for storing tweets in a database. (Ironically, Twitter stores tweets internally as SQL objects. See their GitHub page for their implementation, and this Quora conversation for more information.) The Social Media and Political Participation Lab at New York University, for example, stores its tweets in MongoDB databases. MongoDB is open source and can be used through R or Python.

Databases may not be necessary, however. Their advantages over flat files dominate when the object to be scanned is too large to fit into the memory or computing time is a constraining factor, neither of which are as large an impediment as they may originally seem. First, a day's tweets require approximately 12 gigabytes, and high-performance laptops commonly have 16 gigabytes of RAM; processing and compressing the tweets after they are downloaded makes them even smaller. Desktops commonly have 32 or 64 gigabytes of RAM, and a server much more. Second, the connection to Twitter can be maintained in such a way as to minimize the size of flat files. For example, my connections to Twitter's API restart every hour, meaning I have one file per hour of tweets. These files are 500 megabytes raw, 33 subsetted and compressed, and it is trivial to read a file that size into memory.

Though individual files may be small, you are likely to want to read many of them to find tweets of interest. For example, I have downloaded tweets since August 26, 2013 and frequently want to scan the 365*24*(number of days since then) files for tweets from a particular country. A database could do this quickly. But it is trivial to write a script to scan these files and pull the tweets that are from a country (or match any other criteria in which I am interested). How long this script takes will depend on how many files exist, how they are loaded into memory, and if the code runs in parallel. My script takes a few days to scan every file, but it is rare that I need to read every file; the vast majority of files can be ignored based on their date

Computing time is inexpensive, and there are always other tasks to focus on in the meantime. Once the subset of tweets matching my criteria are found, the equivalent of the results of a database query, subsequent analysis can proceed much more quickly.

## 4  Clean and Analyze

This section provides scripts and examples for cleaning and analyzing tweets. Whether purchased, downloaded from the REST API, or acquired through the streaming API, raw tweets require processing in order to conduct most analyses. For example, tweets from both APIs are formatted in JSON, a convenient data structure that is not rectangular and therefore difficult to be analyzed without transformation; Sifter delivers tweets as a spreadsheet but with oddly named columns and a timestamp that needs conversion.

Section 4.1 explains how to clean data from Sifter, the REST API, and the streaming and provides scripts to do that. Section 4.2 shows how to evaluate tweets for hashtags, non-hashtag keywords, retweets, user mentions, links, and language. Section 4.3 demonstrates, with an example from Bahrain, that tweets can be also used for event detection. Section 4.4 discusses analyzing data contained in links users tweet; these links can point to articles or an image the user has shared. Section 4.5 explains how to generate data outside of the context of the tweet text. Twitter delivers user metadata with a tweet, and the researcher can generate other metadata via, for example, events and census datasets.

### *4.1  Clean*

#### 4.1.1  Tweets from Sifter

I purchased tweets from 21 accounts in Egypt and Bahrain over a three-month period in early 2011; the accounts generated 55,849 tweets in that period. The raw tweets from Egypt are here (www.cambridge.org/download_file/949164). Due to Twitter's terms of service, readers interested in obtaining the raw tweets from Bahrain should contact the author. Note that the column names at that link have been cleaned from how Sifter delivers them; this section will show you how to clean the column names.

Sifter provides its data in data frame format as a comma separated file, so it is easy to load into memory. The header of the data frame is clear, but many of the fields are formatted awkwardly, are unnecessary, or both. For example, the tweet text is repeated twice, with one of the columns called "Title", and there is also a column that shows the parameters submitted to Sifter. A majority of the columns also start with "X.M.." and end with "..", e.g. "X.M ... followers_count.." This R script (www.cambridge.org/download_ file/949161) reads a data frame from Sifter, modifies the header, and writes a new file containing two less columns than the original. This Python script (www.cambridge.org/download_file/949158) does the same.

The script also corrects each tweet's timestamp. Twitter reports all times based on Greenwich Mean Time so the script adjusts forward two hours for Egyptian tweets, three for Bahraini ones. To do that it, it cleans how Sifter provides the timestamp. This cleaning had already been performed on the Bahrain dataset and Egypt dataset used later; the clean Egypt dataset is here (www .cambridge.org/download_file/949155).

### 4.1.2   Tweets from the REST API
Since Twitter does not permit the sharing of more than 50,000 tweets per day, it may not always be possible to obtain a corpus of tweets as easily as clicking on the links in the previous section. Instead, it is more likely that you will have to download the tweets using their tweet identification numbers; Twitter allows the unlimited sharing of these. This section describes how to do that.

The process is the same as the one introduced in the scripts for downloading specific tweets from the REST API (www.cambridge .org/download_file/949143), and this file shows it in Python (www .cambridge.org/download_file/949146). The R script at this link (www.cambridge.org/download_file/949143) reads in a set of of tweet IDs (saved from the raw purchased tweets and available at this link (www.cambridge.org/download_file/949140)).

```
 1 tweets <- NULL # Empty object that tweets will feed into
 2 # Download tweets
 3 for(i in 1:length(chunkedTweets)){
 4   print(paste('On cycle', i, 'of', length-
     (chunkedTweets), sep=' ')) # Status tracker
 5   temp <- twListToDF(lookup_statuses(ids =
     chunkedTweets[[i]]))
 6   tweets <- rbind(tweets, temp)
 7   print(c('Pausing'))
 8   Sys.sleep(delay) # How many seconds to pause so that do
     not trip rate limit. Commented out in this loop because
     downloading 3,200 tweets will never exceed the rate
     limit. (60 requests * 100 tweets per request) > 3200
     tweets
 9 }
10 write.csv(tweets, 'Sifter_Twitter_IDs_
   Downloadedtweets.csv')
```

The full script takes you through steps to verify your account with Twitter, load the identification numbers, and calculate the length of the delay based on the rate limit. Because the process is no different than downloading tweets not acquired through Sifter, I have not created a specific Python script for this process; use the Python script for tweets based on their identification number.

Once the tweets are downloaded and put into a data frame, they require further processing to integrate with the scripts developed to analyze Sifter data. This R script (www.cambridge .org/download_file/949137) modifies column names; assigns each tweet to a country; adds variables for hashtags, user mentions, retweets, and the country of the tweet author; and adjusts the time to local time. It then saves the data as `Tweets_Dataframe_Twitter_IDs_Downloadedtweets_Cle-aned.csv`. This Python script does the same (www.cambridge

.org/download_file/949134). The scripts in the next section will now work on data either obtained from Sifter or downloaded via the REST API and twitteR.

### 4.1.3    Tweets from the Streaming API

Tweets downloaded from the streaming API also require some processing before they can be used for analysis. streamR preserves the raw JSON tweet when it writes files, and it converts them to a data frame with the parseTweets() function. However, parseTweets() does not preserve every entity (retweets, user mentions, or hashtags), so those need to be manually recreated. You could load the raw text file where each tweet is a JSON object, but R does not have robust packages for reading JSON data.

This R script (www.cambridge.org/download_file/949125) does that. It reads tweets saved via streamR's sampleStream() or filterStream() functions, renames columns for consistency with other scripts in this Element, and flags tweets with hashtags, that are retweets, or that mention a user. It also formats the tweet creation time field. This Python script (www.cambridge.org/download_file/949134) does the same except it reads JSON-formatted tweets.

If you elect to save the tweets in their native JSON format and want to use R, the easiest way to convert them to .csv files is to use the csvkit toolkit. csvkit is a command line utility that works on Apple or Linux machines. It has a command, csvjson, that converts a JSON file to a .csv one. You can then load that .csv with read.csv. In Python, you can read the JSON file with the json library or use the pandas library's read_json function to read the JSON file as a dataframe.

Remember, nothing dictates that the data frames containing the tweets be formatted as laid out in the proceeding three scripts. They were done this way for consistency with each other so that subsequent analytical scripts do not have to account for the source of the tweet. Modify the scripts to your preferences.

## 4.2 Text Analysis

Twitter is most commonly used as a platform for gathering text data. This section provides code for common Twitter text analysis tasks such as counting hashtags, non-hashtag keywords, retweets, user mentions, link sharing, and language frequency. It will also show how to estimate whether tweets come from mobile or desktop devices, as well as which kind of mobile device. Tweets can be pooled across any time period; these analyses will aggregate by the hour to show average patterns in these behaviors. The Sifter data will again be used.

The following extracts are only of R scripts. Each R script adds metadata (about hashtags or links or user mentions, for example) and plots the resulting trends. Graphing in R is much easier (and prettier) than in Python, so I did not replicate these scripts in Python. Instead, I created this Python script (www.cambridge.org/download_file/949122) that cleans JSON-formatted tweets, adds metadata, and writes these new data as a .csv file. It adds metadata for each situation described below. If you prefer that script to the R version, you will still need the second half of each R script to aggregate and plot the metadata.

When Twitter sends a JSON formatted tweet, it has already extracted the hashtags and created a field in the tweet object that lists each hashtag. Sifter converts this information to a column where each entry is an empty string (no hashtags in the tweet) or a string with a semi-colon separating each hashtag. This processing saves the analyst a few steps. This script (www.cambridge .org/download_file/949116) creates variables to count tweets with at least one hashtag as well as the number of hashtags in each tweet. It then aggregates by country-hour and generates four plots, which are shown in Figures 1–4. The key lines are:

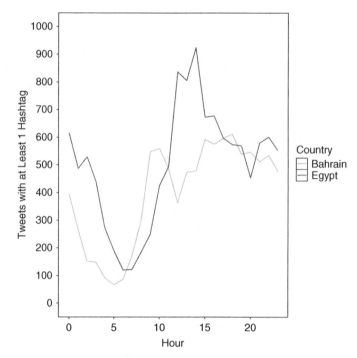

**Figure 1.** Tweets with hashtag

```
1 data$hashtag_dummy <- ifelse(nchar(data$hashtag) == 0,
   0, 1)
2 data$hashtag_count <- apply(as.matrix(data$hashtag),
   MAR=1, FUN = function(x) ifelse(nchar(x) == 0, 0, length
   (unlist(strsplit(x, ';')))))  # If the hashtag column
   has length 0, the tweet contains 0 hashtags. If the length
   is not 0, count the number of hashtags by splitting the
   string on the semi-colon; that is where the split occurs
   because Sifter uses the semicolor to separate hashtags.
   apply() does this to each tweet.
3
4 data_hashtagAgg <- as.data.frame(data \%>\% group_by
   (Country, Hour) \%>\% summarize(tweet_with_hashtag =
   sum(hashtag_dummy), tweet_with_hashtag_perc = sum
   (hashtag_dummy)/sum(count), hashtags_per_tweet = mean
   (hashtag_count), conditional_hashtags_per_tweet =
   mean(hashtag_count[hashtag_dummy==1])))
```

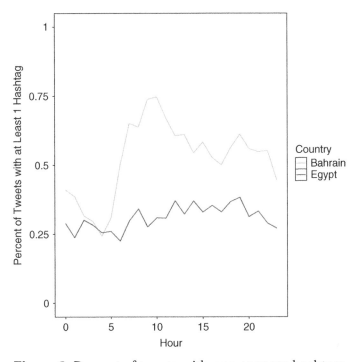

**Figure 2.** Percent of tweets with one or more hashtags

Because a hashtag is simply a word with a symbol prefix, searching a tweet for a particular keyword entails a similar process. Finding a particular keyword is slightly more difficult because neither Twitter nor Sifter process the tweet text for keywords. Finding a particular keyword is useful if you have been collecting a random sample of tweets and become interested in a particular event or term after the tweets are downloaded. Note that the script provides code for English keywords only. The process is the same for non-English tweets, so long as you know the UTF-8 code for the characters that comprise the terms in which you are interested. For more on UTF-8 and R, see R's encoding function, documentation on searching inside a string, and these examples.

The script to find keywords is here (www.cambridge.org/down load_file/949113). These lines show how to search a tweet for a specific keyword:

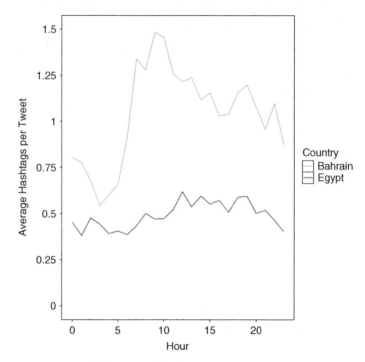

**Figure 3.** Hashtags per tweet

```
1 data$protest <- ifelse(grepl('protest', data$tweet_-
  text, ignore.case = TRUE) == TRUE, 1,0) # If a tweet con-
  tains the word "protest", assign a 1. Case insensitive.
2 data$police <- ifelse(grepl('police', data$tweet_text,
  ignore.case = TRUE) == TRUE, 1, 0) # If a tweet contains the
  word police, assign a 1.
3
4 data$jan25 <- ifelse(grepl('jan25', data$tweet_text,
  ignore.case = TRUE) == TRUE, 1,0)
5 data$feb14 <- ifelse(grepl('feb14', data$tweet_text,
  ignore.case = TRUE) == TRUE, 1,0)
6
7 data$egypt <- ifelse(grepl('egypt', data$tweet_text,
  ignore.case = TRUE) == TRUE, 1,0)
8 data$bahrain <- ifelse(grepl('bahrain', data$tweet_-
  text, ignore.case = TRUE) == TRUE,1,0)
```

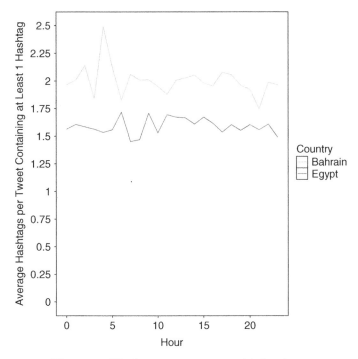

**Figure 4.** Hashtags per tweet with hashtag

Note that this script will find when that word is a hashtag ("Let's go #protest") and stands on its own ("Let's go protest"). The script then aggregates and plots these words. Figure 5 shows the result.

Finding a tweet with a link is a similar process to finding a keyword. Instead of looking for a whole word, however, you can look for "http://". The key line then becomes:

```
1 data$link <- ifelse(grepl('http://', data$tweet_text,
    ignore.case = TRUE) == TRUE, 1,0) # If a tweet contains
    http, assume that is a link. Case insensitive.
```

This script (www.cambridge.org/download_file/949110) contains the code to identify links and generate a plot of the percentage of tweets with links by country–hour. That output is shown in Figure 6.

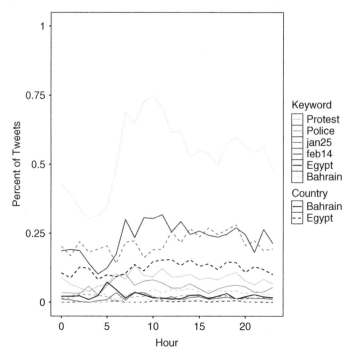

**Figure 5.** Keywords

Finding retweets should be done two ways. First, Twitter identifies a retweet with the retweeted key in the JSON formatted tweet. Sifter translates that to the "is_retweet" column with Boolean flags; the script to clean Sifter data converts those flags into a dummy variable. Second, you should read each tweet for the "RT" characters, paying attention to capitalization. Twitter only identifies a retweet if a user has used Twitter's interface to retweet a tweet (a "native retweet"), but users sometimes retweet by typing "RT @<screen name of tweet creator>" and pasting the copied tweet. Since Twitter does not flag these tweets as retweets, a manual check ensures all retweets are found. In the Sifter sample, only 501 tweets are native retweets, but 12,717 contain "RT ". Figure 7 shows this difference, and the full script for identifying retweets is at this link (www.cambridge.org/down load_file/949107). The key line is this:

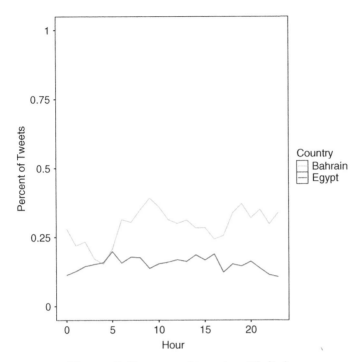

**Figure 6.** Percent of tweets with links

```
1 data$retweet_manual_ignoreCase <- ifelse(grepl('RT_@'
    data$tweet_text, ignore .case = TRUE) == TRUE, 1, 0)
```

Like hashtags, Twitter treats user mentions as an "entity", meaning it extracts the screen names of those a tweet mentioned before delivering that tweet via its API. This processing saves the researcher from using regular expressions, facilitating analyzing the data. Sifter takes the extract screen names and creates a column called `user_mention_username` where each value is one string containing each username mentioned in the tweet. Processing these data is similar to finding hashtags. The script for user mentions is here (www.cambridge.org/download_file/949104), and the key lines are:

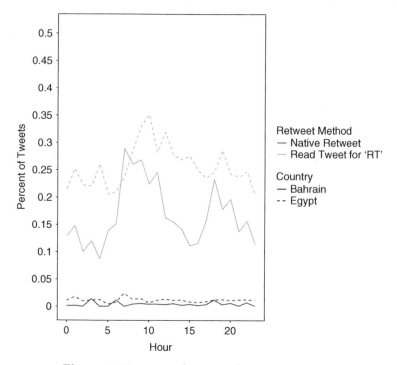

**Figure 7.** Percent of tweets that are retweets

```
1 data$mention_dummy <- ifelse(nchar(data$user_mentio-
  n_username) == 0, 0, 1)
2 data$mention_count <- apply(as.matrix(data$user_mentio-
  n_username), MAR = 1, FUN = function(x) ifelse(nchar(x) ==
  0, 0, length(unlist(strsplit(x, '; ')))))
  # If the Sifter mention column has length 0, the tweet con-
  tains 0 user mentions. If the length is not 0, count the
  number of mentions by splitting the string on the semi-
  colon; that is where the split occurs because Sifter uses
  the semi-color to separate user mentions. apply () does
  this to each tweet.
3
4 # Specific user mentioned? Use @ZacharyST as example
5 sum(grepl('ZacharyST', data$tweet_text, ignore.case =
  TRUE)) # 0.
```

I leave it to the reader to create the user mention figures. I will provide the figures upon request, if you would like to check your work.

Twitter also labels a tweet with the language it is written in, using the language's two letter IS0-639-1 code. Sifter, however, does not convey this information, so you need to recreate it. In R, the best way is through the `textcat` package, which uses the character based n-gram methodology developed in Cavnar and Trenkle (1994). The script to assign language is here (www.cambridge.org /download_file/949101), and the key lines are:

```
1 data$language <- apply(as.matrix(data$tweet_text),
    MARGIN = 2, FUN = function(x) textcat(x))
2
3 data$language[is.na(data$language)] <- 'arabic'
    # Convert the NA to Arabic
4
5 data$english <- as.numeric(ifelse(data$language ==
    'english', 1, 0))
6 data$arabic <- as.numeric(ifelse(data$language != 'eng-
    lish', 1, 0)) # Assumes all non-English tweets are Arabic
```

Figure 8 shows the distribution of languages by country-hour. Note that `textcat()` does not work well on Arabic text and confuses many English tweets for Gaelic or Scottish English. To account for this misassignment, the script manually recategorizes some languages. It also puts most of the languages into an "Other" category, to facilitate visualization.

Finally, Twitter provides metadata on the source of the tweet. The metadata are a string such as "http://www.twitter.com" or "Twitter for iPhone", and Sifter rewrites those strings so that they are clearer. Table 2 shows the distribution of these sources in the Sifter dataset, and Figure 9 shows the distribution of these sources by country–hour. Note that I have categorized the sources by whether or not they are mobile devices or not. The code to generate the table and figure is here (www.cambridge.org/download_file/ 949098), and the key lines are:

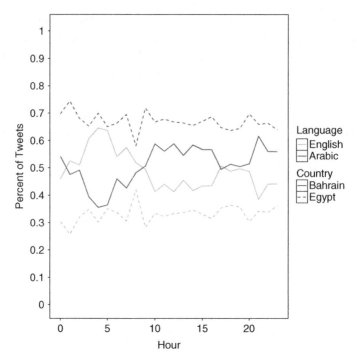

**Figure 8.** Percent of tweets by language

```
1 xtable(as.table(sort(table(data$source), decreasing =
    TRUE))) # Outputs latex table
2
3 desktop <- c ('web', 'Choqok', 'TweetDeck', 'HootSuite',
    'Ping.fm') # The sources most likely to be from a desktop
    computer
4 data$desktop <- ifelse(data$source \%in\% desktop, 1, 0)
5 data$mobile <- ifelse(!(data$source \%in\% desktop),
    1, 0)
```

**Table 2** Frequency of tweet sources in activist data

|  | Tweet source |
| --- | --- |
| Choqok | 22285 |
| web | 17424 |
| Twitter for BlackBerry⸱⸱ | 5142 |
| Twitter for iPhone | 4157 |
| Gravity | 2003 |
| †berSocial | 1977 |
| Facebook | 741 |
| HootSuite | 614 |
| TweetDeck | 353 |
| Snaptu | 344 |
| twitterfeed | 282 |
| Ping.fm | 178 |
| Tweet Button | 148 |
| Samsung Mobile | 45 |
| Twitter for iPad | 32 |
| Google | 27 |
| oauth:173069 | 21 |
| Mobile Web | 17 |
| harassmap.org | 13 |
| Bambuser | 11 |
| TwitLonger Beta | 10 |
| Yfrog | 8 |
| TweetMeme | 5 |
| Twitpic | 4 |
| The BOBs | 3 |
| See Who Viewed Your Profile | 2 |
| My Tweet Lovers | 1 |
| oauth:3294 | 1 |
| StumbleUpon iPhone | 1 |

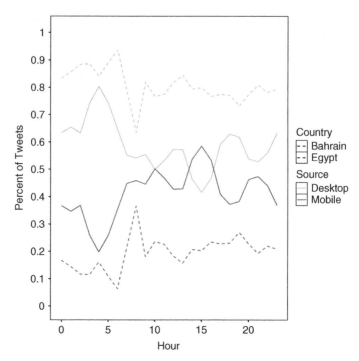

**Figure 9.** Percent of Tweets by Country-Source

## 4.3   Event Detection

Twitter can also be used to generate events data. In the field of political conflict, scholars of subnational conflict rely on events data for theory testing. Events data are datasets that use sources such as non-governmental organization reports (Davenport and Ball, 2002), military records (Weidmann, 2014), or, most commonly, newspaper articles (Metternich *et al.*, 2013; Weidmann and Ward, 2010) to record political interaction between two actors. These sources have known common problems, however, from poor geographic resolution (Hammond and Weidmann, 2014), urban bias (Weidmann, 2014), a preference for unexpected novelty, and, for newspapers, bias towards local elites who can interlocute with reporters (Kalyvas, 2004).

The current best practice uses machine coding of newspaper articles to measure daily events; examples include GDELT, Phoenix (its open source improvement), and ICEWS (Leetaru and Schrodt, 2013; Analytics, 2015; Boschee *et al.*, 2015). These datasets are a significant improvement over previous work because they are updated daily and can draw on one to two orders of magnitude more data sources. They still suffer, however, from the same bias as hand-coded datasets. Analyses based on these databases are therefore still likely to underreport ongoing events (Masad, 2013) or those outside of cities (Weidmann, 2014).

Tweets complement the current state-of-the-art in four ways. First, focusing on individual accounts means one should be able to observe events that would not otherwise appear in events data. Second, these events should exhibit less of an urban bias. Third, even within cities, they allow interested parties to see events with a greater geographic resolution, e.g. a tweet may report on a march in a specific neighborhood or an attack on a police station. For example, events at the city-level, e.g. a protest in Central Park and another in Wall Street, would count as one protest in existing datasets but two in a Twitter events dataset. Fourth, a decrease in interest may result in a smaller decrease in signal: so long as these events are relevant to some people, they should appear in a dataset for longer than they would in datasets that rely on newspapers.

To explore this possibility, I worked with two students to generate events data from a subset of the tweets provided in the Bahrain Sifter tweets (provided upon request). Two undergraduates from the University of California, San Diego have manually coded tweets from human rights activists in Bahrain spanning February 14, 2011 through March 17 of the same year, the height of Arab Spring protests in Bahrain. I then aggregated and deduplicated their coding in order to compare the Twitter results to ICEWS; the ICEWS data are contained at this link (www.cambridge.org/download_file/949095).

Figure 10 shows that events from these tweets reveal patterns that are noticeably different than those of ICEWS, the dataset to which

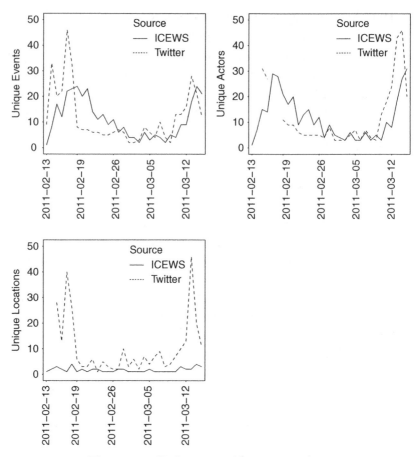

**Figure 10.** Twitter provides events data

I compare them. The tweets record events across many more locations than ICEWS, an average of 20 per day versus three for ICEWS.
For example, the tweets record clashes in suburbs such as Duraz or
outlying cities such as Sanabis, and there are two reports of nerve
gas used against protestors. Within Manama, clashes are recorded
at the airport, Dana Mall, and Bahrain University, among other
places too precise for ICEWS to reference. Other locations include
an activist's home and Sitra, Bahrain's seventh largest city.
The tweets also record more actors than ICEWS, an average of 25

versus 12. The tweets record a similar number of events as ICEWS, though it does record more events at the start of Bahrains protests.

In addition to recording more locations and actors than ICEWS, the Twitter events data record different patterns of activity. ICEWS records a spike in actors at the beginning and end of the period containing the tweets, with a lull in the middle (late February to mid-March). The tweets record the same pattern, but with greater spikes at the beginning and end of the sample period; from late February to mid-March, the tweets record the same number of actors as ICEWS. Most interestingly, ICEWS records the same number of locations throughout the sample period. The tweets, on the other hand, show a u-shape: events happen in more locations at the beginning and end of the protest period, with few locations recording events from late February to early March. In other words, ICEWS appears to record events in the same areas over time. Overall, events data from Twitter appear to report more actors engaging in more activity across more locations than current best practice data suggest.

The code to generate events data and the figures is here (www .cambridge.org/download_file/949086), and the handcoded datasets are here (www.cambridge.org/download_file/949083) and here (www.cambridge.org/download_file/949080).

The code is meant purely as a proof of concept. Its geocoding relies on human-identified places in tweets, and the same place is often spelled multiple ways. Only English tweets were coded. The limits of English compared to local language tweets is probably real, but it is unknown; they are certainly not as limited as English newspapers. Most importantly, a real-time dataset that records multiple kinds of events across the globe and with intracity resolution cannot be created by humans. An eventual system would need to be fully automated, and this script does not start the learning process that would create a classifier for a final product.

## 4.4   Links and Imagery

It is common for users to share links in their tweets. The content of links is a potentially rich source of information for researchers, but they remain understudied. The most common way links are analyzed is for researchers to note the percentage of tweets containing them (Suh *et al.*, 2010; Steinert-Threlkeld, 2017a), but I am aware of no articles that analyze the content of those links. There are two reasons links remain understudied.

First, spam accounts tweet links. The presence of a link, in conjunction with age of an account and the use of trending topics, is a common way researchers identify spam accounts (Kwak *et al.*, 2010). While bots may represent 6% to 8.4% of all accounts, it is unknown what percentage of links they share (Lotan *et al.*, 2011); it is probably more. (Not all bots are spam accounts, but I am not aware of any work which manually identifies spam accounts.) Astroturf political campaigns commonly use authentic looking accounts controlled by a political operation to share one or a few links, creating the appearance of a grassroots concern where none exists (Mustafaraj and Metaxas, 2010; Ratkiewicz *et al.*, 2011). Without a reliable, precise spam filter, a researcher studying links risks studying spam.

Second, studying links requires additional processing work. When Twitter delivers a tweet with a link, it extracts the link for the downloader. It does not, however, deliver the content contained at the link. Theoretically, you could estimate the link's content by reading the URL, as newspaper links often contain the headline. Twitter, however, automatically shortens links; while useful to the tweet creator, the shortening means information the full URL contains is removed, and the researcher has to follow the link to the webpage. A researcher interested in link content therefore has to build a web crawling system on top of the one connecting to Twitter.

The most compelling reason to study links is because they often point to images, and image analysis is a new frontier of machine learning. Twitter is traditionally text focused, but imagery is becoming the most popular content shared on social networks. Images are commonly shared on Twitter, including images containing more than 140 characters of text. I am aware of no study which quantifies what percentage of tweets contain imagery, though a few studies have analyzed images on Twitter. Kaneko *et al.* (2013) use geo-tagged tweets with photos to detect sporting events and even fireworks. Mehrdad Yazdani and Lev Manovich (2015) correlate 1 million images from 20 United States cities over one year with self-reported measures of happiness as well as socio-economic indicators.

Image analysis for the social sciences is still in its infancy, however, because computational requirements for images are higher. Image files are much larger than text files, and feature detection is more complicated. It is relatively easy to create variables (features) from text, but determining which parts of an image file represent quantities of interest (people or places, for example) is much harder. Recent advances in neural networks, colloquially now called "deep learning", are promising, but these models require extremely powerful computers and generate classifications in ways that make the features determining those classifications difficult to understand. If a tweet contains an image, Twitter provides the link to the image but not to the image itself; the researcher must then add this processing step to the data acquisition pipeline. I am aware of only one paper which uses images to answer a political question, and it is still a working paper (Anastasopoulos *et al.*, 2016). One paper, a conference proceeding, analyzes images shared on Twitter to detect and measure characteristics fo protests (Won, Steinert-Threlkeld, and Joo 2017).

Satellite imagery is a promising subset of image analysis and the one most likely to be incorporated first in analyses. Images of light have already been used to measure economic development, for example. Because Earth's colors and geographic features are more stable than random photos from a social network, the first rigorous use of image data in the social sciences will probably come from satellite imagery. Currently, these images are best for cross-sectional analysis, as satellites pass over places irregularly.

## 4.5  Enriching Tweets

You can enrich the information in a tweet's text in four ways. If conducting text analysis, any of these approaches enable a structural topic model (Roberts *et al.*, 2014).

First, you can consult the metadata Twitter provides with a tweet. These data include how many followers the author has, how many accounts the author follows, when the account was created, the account's default language, the language of the tweet, and if the tweet has GPS coordinates, among others. The user's self-reported location is provided in approximately 50% of tweets (Leetaru and Schrodt, 2013), and individuals commonly make their screen name the same as, or similar to, their real name (Barberá *et al.*, 2015a).

Second, you could also interview the individuals behind an account. Two difficulties arise. First, messaging an account requires that the recipient follows the sending account. In other words, survey respondents have to first follow the survey adminis- trator, which is unrealistic. Second, interviewing would require Institutional Review Board (IRB) approval. A more expeditious approach is to interview people and ask if they use Twitter (Tufekci and Wilson, 2012; Zickuhr, 2013).

Third, accounts' tweeting patterns and social network can reveal information not in tweets' text. For example, accounts belonging to unemployed individuals have tweets more during the day, and cities with higher levels of unemployment have low communica- tion entropy (Llorente *et al.*, 2014). The style of tweets gives some indication of an account's age (Nguyen *et al.*, 2013). Social class, ethnicity, and education can be estimated probabilistically when tweets contain GPS coordinates (Malik *et al.*, 2015). A user's social network is also more predictive of that user's age and political affiliation than relying on just user attributes (Zamal *et al.*, 2012). These techniques are compelling, but there exists no R or Python packages that implement them automatically, increasing the costs of their use. A researcher may have to reinvent the wheel each time; the need for such data should be great before time is invested in this approach.

Finally, you can manually inspect each account in a sample. By viewing a profile's photo, gender may be obvious, and an age range could be created. An account's past tweets can give an indica- tion of the author's primary location and interests. Googling the account name may reveal other sites where the author has registered, and those sites may provide more demographic information. This manual approach is what Driscoll and Steinert-Threlkeld (2017) use to assign occupation, age, and gender to the accounts in their sample. To create data on enough accounts for a quantitative study using this approach requires cheap human labor.

Another enrichment involves connecting aggregated Twitter data to other datasets. For example, Twitter users can sometimes be found in voter files or campaign donation contribution datasets; this approach has been used to validate political inferences made from individual's network (Barberá, 2015). Inferences can be made about tweets aggregated to census tract levels, both in the United States (Mislove *et al.*, 2011; Malik *et al.*, 2015) and elsewhere (Sloan *et al.*, 2015). Tweets aggregated to the country level can also be connected to events datasets (Steinert-Threlkeld *et al.*, 2015; Steinert-Threlkeld, 2017a).

Other datasets entice. With the recent release of IRS 990 filings, it may be possible to link Twitter accounts to charitable donations to non-profit organizations. For example, it would be interesting to see if the ideal points of non-profit organizations correlates with the ideal points of their donors. While reliable census data tend to come from wealthy countries, countries such as the Philippines, Turkey, and Ukraine have disaggregated census data that have not been combined with Twitter data.

## 5   Twitter in the Social Sciences

This section provides examples of applications other social scientists have made of Twitter data. It also summarizes competitors to the platform – Facebook, Reddit, Sina Weibo, Tumblr, and Instagram – as well as the potential of call detail record (CDR) data (https://en.wikipedia.org/wiki/Call_detail_record).

### 5.1   *Research on Social Media*

The speed of academic publishing in the social sciences means that papers taking advantage of Twitter data have only started to appear after 2010 (Twitter was founded in 2006). The appeal of Twitter, and "big data" more broadly, is that it provides data on more people in more places across more time than scholars could realistically hope to achieve with survey methods. For example, it has long been known that individuals' happiness is lowest during the middle of the day, and lower during the week than on weekends; the cost of acquiring data meant these results were only tested in WEIRD (Western, educated, industrialized, rich, and democratic) countries (Henrich *et al.*, 2010), but Twitter reveals that it applies in at least 84 countries (Golder and Macy, 2011). Countries also experience similar changes in their total happiness, though baseline levels vary (Poblete *et al.*, 2011). Because people use social media to talk about topics such as health, these platforms can also be used to monitor public health and identify individuals susceptible to treatment (Charles-Smith *et al.*, 2015).

In political science, Twitter has been used in two main areas of research: conflict dynamics and public opinion. For an early review of social media and social movements, see the 2013 special issue of *American Behavioral Scientist* called "New Media and Social Unrest" (Tufekci and Freelon, 2013). For a review of the potential and challenges of using online social network platforms for research, see Golder and Macy (2014). For a series of essays on the role of big data in the social sciences, see the 2015 symposium in *PS: Political Science and Politics* titled "Big Data, Causal Inference, and Formal Theory: Contradictory Trends in Political Science?" (www .cambridge.org/core/journals/ps-political-science-and-politics /issue/F71EE285BFB51E27DCE368E94D5A0F8B).

Thomas Zeitzoff has three papers that show how Twitter can generate new insights into conflict and foreign policy. Because the costs of posting on Twitter are much lower than for publishing in a newspaper or broadcasting on television, individuals and small organizations have become sources of events data. Zeitzoff (2011) combines @AJGaza (an Al-Jazeera Twitter account) and @QassamCount (a record of rocket attacks into Israel) tweets with blog reports and a Wikipedia event timeline to examine the microdynamics of Israel's 2009 war in Gaza, finding that:

Hamas's and Israel's response intensity double immediately after the introduction of ground troops and that immediately following the UN Security Council vote, Israel cuts its response intensity in half, while Hamas's slightly increases. (p. 939)

This paper appears to be the earliest incorporation of social media data into conflict studies.

Aday *et al.* (2012), in a report for the United States Institute of Peace (USIP), present another early use of Twitter in the social sciences. In a similar report for the USIP from 2010, many of the same authors proposed a framework for analyzing the effect of online media on contentious politics. Their data, however, was limited to a case study of digital media during Iran's 2009 protests (Aday *et al.*, 2010). They examine the geographic distribution of individuals clicking on bit.ly links in tweets and find that:

new media informs international audiences and mainstream media reporting rather than plays a direct role in organizing protests or allowing local audiences to share self-generated news directly with one another. ... The key role of new media may be its bridging function: from an activist core to mass publics, from user-generated content to mainstream mass media, and from local struggles to international attention. (p. 5)

Later work uses Twitter to study protest mobilization directly. Combining geolocated tweets with computer-generated events data, scholars have found that the more the peripheral members of a country's social network tweet about protests, the more subsequent protests there are (Steinert-Threlkeld *et al.*, 2015; Steinert-Threlkeld, 2017b). A study comparing the Twitter network of people who protested in Paris after the *Charlie Hebdo* attacks with those who did not, found that protestors and non-protestors segregate on Twitter (Larson *et al.*, 2016).

Twitter also reveals how social networks vary by country. Zeitzoff *et al.* (2015) show how follower relationships on Twitter provide social network data that can be used to infer issue salience (Zeitzoff *et al.*, 2015). Combining users tweeting in English, Farsi, and Arabic with network analysis of Farsi and Arabic blogs, the authors show that users separate into identifiable ideological clusters. However, network topology varies depending on which set of users is considered.

Twitter can also reveal daily changes in the social network of its users. In Egypt and Bahrain, over a three-month period in early 2011, the two countries' Twitter networks become more similar and a multitude of communities arose which bridged communities in both countries (Steinert-Threlkeld, 2017a).

Not only can Twitter (and social media more broadly) provide data on events in a conflict, it may influence conflicts directly. The percentage of protestors at Egypt's Tahrir Square who heard about the protests on social media was much higher than the percentage of Egyptians on Twitter (Tufekci and Wilson, 2012). In Russia's 2011 parliamentary elections, users of Twitter and Facebook were more likely to believe electoral fraud occurred, while users of indigenous social network sites did not have that perception (Reuter and Szakonyi, 2013); the direction of causality is unclear, however. In Ukraine, early participants in the Euromaidan protests were much more likely to have learned about the protests via Facebook than the later protests (Onuch, 2015). See Bastos *et al.* (2015) for an analysis of Twitter and Facebook during the global Occupy movement, May 15, and Vinegar protest movements in Brazil. In Israel's 2012 conflict with Gaza, both sides varied their attack intensity based on international public opinion, where public opinion is measured as the number of times a pro-Israel or pro-Hamas hashtag is used per hour (Zeitzoff, 2016). While a potential causal role for social media is still hotly debated, there now exists a critical mass of work in this domain that suggests further theoretical and empirical development is warranted (Tucker *et al.*, 2016). For an example of Twitter being used to exogenously induce mobilization (in support for an online petition), see Coppock *et al.* (2016). For the best causal identification yet of the extent to which social media may lead to larger protests, see Enikolopov et al. (2016)'s study of VKontakte and Russia's 2011 protests.

Another domain in which social media and Twitter have allowed scholars to make advances is in measuring political preferences. For example, many scholars worry that digital communications technology allows individuals to consume information which reinforces already held opinions (Adamic and Glance, 2005; Farrell, 2012). Early studies using Twitter find that retweet networks sort on ideological preference while user mention networks do not (Conover *et al.*, 2011, 2012).

A limitation of these studies, however, is that ideology is manually inferred based on the topic of the tweet, making the results difficult to scale. A more recent advance is to observe which political accounts Twitter users follow; these relationships place individuals in latent political space that closely matches what DW-NOMINATE would assign, making it possible to estimate millions of individuals' otherwise unobservable political preferences (Barberá, 2015). Research using this method has found evidence of ideological exchange: while polarization exists, it varies by topic, and ideological communities are not hermetic. It appears that, in the United States, the less political a topic is, such as a sporting event or entertainment news, the more news flows across ideological boundaries; even for political news 12–60% of retweets are from users on opposite sides of the political spectrum (Barberá *et al.*, 2015a). A study of the United States, Spain, and Germany makes an even stronger claim: 33–45% of the accounts Twitter users follow are from the opposite side of the political spectrum, and individuals become more moderate over time as their network becomes more politically diverse (Barberá, 2014). On Facebook, individuals who report whether they are liberal or conservative have approximately 20% of their friends from across the aisle, and 22–30% of the news they see contravenes their politics (Bakshy *et al.*, 2015). Interestingly, Barberá (2015) finds that conservatives have fewer cross-cutting ties than liberals, while Bakshy *et al.* (2015) find the opposite.

Because Twitter is popular with politicians, it also provides insight into how they and their constituents interact. Early work looking at how members of Congress use Twitter finds that male

Republican House members tweet the most, with Senators tweeting less than Representatives, and tweeting increased with the length of time in office; for all members of Congress, tweets are used to broadcast policy positions but not to rally public action (Hemphill *et al.*, 2013). When running for office, female candidates have more followers and tweet more than male candidates, while both major parties use the platform similarly (Evans *et al.*, 2014). Later work uses the 354,860 tweets sent by the members of Congress between January 1, 2013 and March 15, 2014 to their follower network, and a random sample of the tweets of those followers finds that legislators are more responsive to their most partisan constituents (though Democrats also respond to non-Democrat constituents), while constituents do not change the topics of their tweets based on legislators' tweets (Barberá *et al.*, 2014).

A cottage industry exists that uses Twitter to predict voting and stock market outcomes. The title of one of the earliest papers is explanatory enough: "Twitter Mood Predicts the Stock Market" (Bollen *et al.*, 2011); using tweets from ten months in 2008, that paper finds that some aggregate measures of mood correlates with changes in the Dow Jones Industrial Average up to six days in the future. Later work finds similar correlation at an hourly level (Zheludev *et al.*, 2014). Researchers have found that the number of mentions of political parties correlates positively with those parties' electoral success in Germany (Tumasjan *et al.*, 2010). For an exhaustingly thorough catalogue of how Twitter has been used to study politics, see Jungherr (2014).

Twitter also provides "polling" for places otherwise difficult to survey, especially when longitudinal analysis is required. For example, following certain users can allow scholars to construct panel data that may reveal changes in a society's beliefs. In Egypt, 17 million tweets from 7,000 users in Egypt have been used to measure discourse polarization, and polarization on Twitter increased before violent protests in November 2012 (Weber *et al.*, 2013). Borge-Holthoefer *et al.* (2015) analyze 6 million Arabic tweets from Egypt from the middle of 2013. With data on 120,000 users and their 3,200 previous tweets, a classifier for pro- or anti-military tweets, and known secular or Islamist accounts, the authors show that few users, never more than 3% on any given day, express views that contradict their previous preferences as expressed on Twitter (Borge-Holthoefer *et al.*, 2015). Twitter can be used to measure pro-Ukraine and pro-Russia sentiment from the start of the protests and in Ukraine and through its civil war; because Twitter polling does not require enumerators, it is especially useful in violent areas of the world such as Ukraine's Luhansk and Donetsk oblasts (Driscoll and Steinert-Threlkeld, 2017).

The failure of voter turnout models used to predict the results of the presidential election in the United States in 2016 suggests that many voters are also difficult to survey. If the election result suggests that traditional institutions, such as the political party and media, are not as influential over individuals as previously believed, then data sources which provide direct access to those individuals may become an important source of polling. Republican nominee Donald Trump's personal use of Twitter also defied expectations and galvanized new political actors. That these actors may misrepresent themselves to polsters, if they respond in the first place, but may exhibit more candor online suggests that Twitter may have more relevance for understanding American political behavior than previously thought.

The presidential election also saw the first use of "fake news" on social media platforms, especially Facebook. ("Fake news" refers to articles that appear to detail actual events but are designed instead to generate internet traffic against which advertisements can be sold. They generate traffic with sensationalist headlines.) Because the behavior is so novel, there does not yet exist a method for automatically detecting fake news; in response to post-election backlash, Facebook's solution is to flag questionable articles for independent organizations to verify manually.

While your initial desire may be to remove tweets containing fake news from a dataset, they should be preserved since their presence presents the opportunity to study information flow in all its forms. Just as social media may provide insight into difficult to survey individuals, it may also let us study types of information flows previously unobservable. Before, the only fake news was in tabloids and rumors; now fake news submerses itself in an observable, recordable, and measurable medium. Do fake news items spread differently than true ones? Are they more, less, or as likely to spread as true news items? If they spread, do they stay within homogenous political communities? We will not know how fake news works if we ignore it altogether.

It should be noted that much skepticism exists concerning the ability of Twitter, and social media more broadly, to serve as a polling platform (Tufekci, 2014). While Twitter has more than 300 million global monthly active users and is used by all demographics in the United States, Pew Research has found its users skew towards the young and minorities (Greenwood *et al.*, 2016), while users who tag their tweets with GPS coordinates tend to be higher income, urban, or minorities (Malik *et al.*, 2015). Papers which claim to predict an outcome tend to conflate correlation with prediction, make *post hoc* claims, and half of the Twitter studies conducted before 2013 failed to predict correctly election outcomes (Gayo-Avello, 2013). These shortcomings may reflect the novelty of working with these data, as no agreed-upon methodology exists for selecting users, cleaning tweets, measuring sentiment, or measuring prediction accuracy (Gayo-Avello, 2013). Future work needs to reorient its claims, reweight its samples, and gain external validity by using panel, instead of cross-sectional, data (Diaz *et al.*, 2016).

Finally, Twitter is especially exciting for the study of social networks and mobilization. For example, voter mobilization studies interested in social networks rely on surveys to measure the effect of social networks on voting (Lake and Huckfeldt, 1998; Dalton *et al.*, 2002; Nickerson, 2008). While Nickerson (2008) is able to exogenously assign treatment, most work relies on respondents reporting if their friends vote or share their political preferences. While I am aware of no published research that uses Twitter to mobilize voters, it has been used to mobilize support for online petitions (Coppock *et al.*, 2016). Facebook was used in the 2010

United States Congressional Election to mobilize 340,000 additional voters (Bond *et al.*, 2012). Studies of mobilization in the context of the United States Civil Rights movement (McAdam, 1986) or East Germany's 1989 protests (Opp and Gern, 1993) are similarly reliant on *post hoc* observational survey data. Twitter allows scholars to monitor protests in real time, allowing them to observe for the first time recruitment as it happens (González-Bail ón *et al.*, 2011), the differential effects of individuals in the core and on the periphery of a country's social network (Barberá *et al.*, 2015b; Steinert-Threlkeld, 2017b), and how social network structure affects mobilization (Steinert-Threlkeld, 2017b; Larson *et al.*, 2016).

## 5.2 Competitors

Twitter is unique in its global reach and data availability; it is probably the most studied social network. As of September 21, 2016, a Google Scholar search for "twitter" returns 6,370,000 items, "facebook" 5,390,000, and "instagram" 172,000. Other common platforms are Tumblr (owned by Yahoo), reddit, and Sina Weibo. For a history of social networks and the internet, see Bury *et al.* (2013).

Founded in 2004 for elite US undergraduates, Facebook opened itself to anyone over the age of 13 on September 26, 2006. It is now a major corporation with global market penetration; with over 1 billion users, it is the most popular social network and one of the internet's most visited sites (Bhatia, 2016; Solon, 2016). Facebook was the first social network platform to reach such a large audience, and it quickly drew attention from academics of all disciplines. The first article about it, discussing privacy concerns, appeared in 2005 and analyzed information sharing behaviors of college students (Jones and Soltren, 2005). The ability to observe social connections across large groups of people has drawn the interest of network scientists (Lazer *et al.*, 2009; Gjoka *et al.*, 2010; Ferrara, 2012), physicists and computer scientists (Catanese *et al.*, 2011; Ugander *et al.*, 2011), social scientists

(Lewis *et al.*, 2008; Bond *et al.*, 2012; Reich, Subrahmanyam and Espinoza, 2012), and humanists (Rahimi, 2011). For a review of Facebook studies in the social sciences, see Wilson *et al.* (2012).

Facebook is the juggernaut social network and maintains a well-documented API. The difficulty for researchers is that the vast majority of accounts are private. Facebook initially maintained an internal research team that worked with academics on a broad range of questions, but after an international outcry over one study that showed some users negative, and others positive, news (Kramer *et al.*, 2014), it has become much more cautious in its academic partnerships. Its internal research is now more focused on selling advertisements than it was before that study. Perhaps as part of that turn, only media publishers can access the feed API (the equivalent of Twitter's streaming API). The graph API, which gives information on friendships, is still available.

Reddit, founded in 2005 and now visited by 234 million unique individuals per month, is perhaps the modern platform which least resembles a social network. "The front page of the internet", reddit revolves around subreddits, thematic collections of user-provided material (e.g. photos, questions, essays, links to other stories) that anyone can create or follow. Users vote such material up or down and subscribe to subreddits, but do not connect to other accounts as on a social network. Scholars have paid less attention to the site, with the studies that do exist focusing on attention dynamics (Bergstrom, 2011; Gilbert, 2013; Lakkaraju *et al.*, 2013).

Sina Weibo is the most similar service to Twitter, but it is targeted at users in China. Introduced on August 14, 2009 to replace the recently banned Twitter and Facebook, it has slightly over 200 million active monthly users posting 100 million messages per day. Though open to anyone, only Chinese citizens use it regularly, and there is some concern that its users are fleeing to messaging applications like WeChat and WhatsApp. As with Twitter, many studies focus on event analysis (Qu *et al.*, 2011; Guan *et al.*, 2014), its use during crisis events (Guan *et al.*, 2014), user behavior (Gao *et al.*, 2012; Yu *et al.*, 2012), and spam detection (Yu *et al.*, 2012; Lin *et al.*, 2013; Sun *et al.*, 2013). There is some evidence that Sina Weibo users provide more information about themselves and are more episodic users than individuals on Twitter (Gao *et al.*, 2012). Perhaps the most unique opportunity the platform affords academics is the ability to study censorship in real time and on a scale not possible previously (Hassid, 2012; King *et al.*, 2014, 2016).

Some microblogging competitors to Twitter focus on image sharing. In its capabilities, Tumblr is equivalent to Twitter; in practice, Tumblr is used to share photos and GIFs (short, low-quality videos), with accompanying text. The main difference is that Tumblr does not restrict the length of posts, whereas Twitter restricts them to 140 characters; Twitter was designed with phones in mind, before smart phones existed, and it had to adhere to the character limit available to old phones' text messages. Tumblr is also visually oriented, whereas Twitter has been dominated by text (though Twitter is becoming an image sharing platform as well). Though Tumblr has 555 million monthly active users, it has received less scholarly attention than Twitter (Social, 2016), perhaps because images are more difficult to analyze than text. For structural analysis of the platform, see Chang *et al.* (2014). Xu *et al.* show how the text component of Tumblr can help predict civil wars (Xu *et al.*, 2014), and some works use Tumblr for sentiment analysis (Bourlai and Herring, 2014). There appear to be no published works which analyze the images shared on Tumblr.

Launched in 2010 as a smart phone application, Instagram has become the most popular photo-sharing platform, with over 400 million active users monthly. (Facebook now owns it.) Users post and spread images they produce or find, and text is provided, often with hashtags, on each post. Academics have studied Instagram more than Tumblr but less than Facebook or Twitter. Images provide insight on mass behaviors at specific times and places, as well as on different cultural behaviors (Hochman and Manovich, 2013; Silva *et al.*, 2013). For a structural overview of the Instagram network, see Ferrara *et al.* (2014). For an ontology of users and photographs on the site, see Hu *et al.* (2014). As of November 17, 2015, Instagram does not let third parties (including researchers) access its feed data, which is how you would download posts as they are created.

The best data on offline social networks comes from call detail records, the data telecommunications carriers record on who calls and texts whom, the location of both parties, and the duration of the exchange. Because these data represent actual interactions, they should have more measurement validity than social networks recovered from online social media. A common critique of using social media to study social networks is that one has to assume that the social networks formed online have the same topography as those offline. Call detail records therefore represent a major advance in the measurement of social networks.

The researcher must obtain call detail records on an *ad hoc* basis. No company regularly makes them available, and companies aggregate at different levels of resolution (call or cell phone tower, for example). Orange, the French telecommunications company, has run two "Data 4 Development" competitions where they release call detail records, once from the Ivory Coast and once from Senegal. (They have not announced a regular schedule of competitions.) Finally, a country usually has multiple telecommunications providers, and a research project usually has access to the telecommunications from only one company's.

There exists little published work using call detail records. Nicholas Eubank has used seven months' data from 9 million subscribers to measure ethnic fractionalization in Zambia (Eubank, 2016), and Fotini Christia, Leon Yao, Stephen Wittles, and Jure Leskovec (2015) have started to analyze calls from Yemen during the Arab Spring. Patterns of calls may also predict violence (Berger *et al.*, 2014), and CDR reveal the effect distance has on the probability an individual attends a protest (Traag et al. 2017). Outside of political science, patterns of calling are shown to track international trade but also reflect non-economic behaviors (Blumenstock, 2011), provide insight on international migration (Blumenstock, 2012), predict subnational poverty (Blumenstock *et al.*, 2015), and measure population distribution in real-time and in areas difficult to survey (Douglass *et al.*, 2015).

# 6  Discussion

I conclude by discussing non-programmatic aspects of Twitter. The first section discusses the types of data that tweets do not provide and the limitations thus imposed on analysis. Section 6.2 raises potential ethical concerns of using Twitter data, especially as it relates to minors. I then user behaviors on Twitter to argue that it has features of both a media platform, like newspapers or television, and a social network.

## 6.1  Limitations

While the works referred to above that are skeptical of Twitter enumerate shortcomings of the platform's data, it is worth emphasizing them here as well. The simplest way to summarize these shortcomings is that individual tweets contain little information.

The main reason individual tweets have little information is because they are limited to 140 characters, 20 characters fewer than a text message. (As of November 2017, Twitter has is transitioning to 280 characters per tweet.) As any quick perusal of Twitter reveals, this restriction leads to frequent use of abbreviations; it is also common for a tweet to be a comment on a link shared in the tweet.

What tweets lack in information they make up for in quantity. One tweet may be about football, another music, and another a political candidate; individually, they are not interesting, but aggregated, they reveal interesting patterns about what topics are salient to a given group of people and how that saliency varies by place and time.

One of the drawbacks of Twitter for researchers is one of its appeals for users: anonymity. Registration is free, and registrants can make their screen name any word or phrase they want. Unlike Facebook, then, where you are asked for your first and last name, Twitter will let you appear to the world as "Zachary Steinert-Threlkeld" or "Brown Curtain". While many users choose a screen name that is their name, most do not. Moreover, Twitter does not ask the users their age, education, gender, or race. To overcome this, researchers can take a sample of accounts and manually research them, generating reasonable estimates of the profession, age, gender, and political beliefs of accounts (Lotan *et al.*, 2011; Borge-Holthoefer *et al.*, 2015; Driscoll and Steinert-Threlkeld, 2017). Though much metadata are obtainable via research, such an approach does not scale to large populations.

Twitter users also have to decide to identify their location. They can identify in two ways. First, Twitter asks users their location as part of their profile. Like their user name, however, they can choose any word or phrase they want. While many users choose a real place, as many do not complete this section or give non-sensical answers such as "the sky" or "over there". Second, Twitter users can assign GPS coordinates to their tweets, but they have to choose to do this per tweet; 2–3% of tweets have GPS coordinates attached to them (Leetaru *et al.*, 2013; Budak and Watts, 2015). While a small percentage of tweets contain GPS coordinates, there are 500 million tweets per day. Users who tag their tweets with GPS coordinates do vary from those who do not, but that variation is only understood in the United States (Malik *et al.*, 2015), can be measured in many other countries, and does not necessarily mean the behavior in which the researcher is interested will be biased because the sample is.

To increase the number of geolocated tweets in a sample, scholars infer location based on a user's self-reported location in their profile. Including users' self-reported location, anywhere from 34% (Leetaru *et al.*, 2013) to 50% (Conover *et al.*, 2013) to 66% (Hecht *et al.*, 2011) of tweets have location information, the vast majority of which are at the city level. It is possible to assign location information to accounts based on the context of their tweets (Cheng *et al.*, 2010; Hecht *et al.*, 2011; Stefanidis *et al.* 2011). It is unknown whether accounts with self-reported location differ from those without, so the benefit of this added parsing needs to weighed against the computational cost. The most significant global source of location is an account's time zone, as Twitter automatically assigns a time zone to each tweet based on the location where the tweet author registered (Lotan *et al.*, 2011).

There are two idiosyncrasies to working with tweet text. First, the 140 character limitation means tweets tend to concern themselves with one topic, simplifying analysis. This limitation pushes users towards abbreviations and slang, however, which complicate language processing. Second, tweet style is bimodal, with very many, perhaps a majority, of them using abbreviations and slang. Existing corpora used for dictionary approaches do not include slang, and the idiosyncratic nature of slang means unsupervised approaches are more likely to assign tweets about the same topic to different topics. For a more detailed discussion on natural language processing and Twitter, see Sriram *et al.* (2010) and Han and Baldwin (2011). For a thorough introduction to natural language processing more broadly, see Manning and Schütze (1999).

## 6.2 Ethics

Ethical concerns around the use of Twitter data flow from the scarcity of information in tweets and user profiles.

Because Twitter requires no identifying information to register, it is possible that tweets in a dataset are from children. Because Twitter is a common marketing and branding tool, many products exist which will estimate the demographic age of an account's followers, but age-verification products are expensive on an academics' budget. (Twitter also allows brands to require potential followers to confirm their age before they are allowed to follow.) It is also unknown what percent of users on Twitter are under 18; Pew, which conducts an annual survey of social media usage in America, does not interview minors. While there are studies that estimate the demographic characteristics from the behavior of a Twitter account (Nguyen *et al.*, 2013; Sloan *et al.*, 2015; Sloan and Morgan, 2015), any solutions are not trivial to implement, and I am not aware of any academic Twitter study which attempts to remove minors (or other protected categories) from their samples.

The researcher must also be careful to respect users' desire to delete tweets. If a user deletes a specific tweet, the streaming API will deliver a JSON message with the tweet ID of the now deleted tweet. It is incumbent on the person or group connected to the API to delete the tweet from their data. Twitter is unclear about whether or not the streaming API provides the identification number of all deleted tweets or only a sample of them. Twitter will not make a deleted tweet available via the REST API.

IRBs have not established a common standard for the treatment of Twitter data. When tweets are publicly available and researchers are not conducting interventions, there is no *prima facie* reason studies should need IRB approval. Twitter's public nature has not stopped IRBs from expressing caution about using its data (Halavais, 2011; Hayden, 2013). For a project where my colleague interviewed activists in Egypt and I examined their Twitter behavior, my university's IRB had to approve the fieldwork (Fowler and Steinert-Threlkeld, 2016). When our IRB application mentioned Twitter, they asked for more detail, though Twitter's public nature mollified them.

IRBs' approach to minimally invasive research, such as downloading public data from Twitter, is in flux. On January 19, 2017, United States Government agencies in charge of protecting human subjects issued new guidelines for research that will take effect in January 2018. These guidelines create new exempt categories that require minimal IRB review, and research under these categories does not require continuing review. One of these exempt categories is the "observation and recording of verbal and non-verbal behavior in schools and public places", under which observational Twitter research should fall (Shweder and Nisbett, 2017). How institutions interpret these rules and by how much they lower the administrative cost of research remains to be seen.

While IRBs appear to have adopted an appropriate attitude to observational data from Twitter, there is growing interest in conducting experiments (Coppock *et al.*, 2016; Munger, 2016). Procedures to protect research subjects on Twitter appear to be the same as those for offline experiments. For example, the replication data for Munger (2016) is anonymized and aggregated to the account level so that the accounts targeted with messages cannot be identified. Coppock, Guess and Ternovski (2016) similarly do not share individual tweets, and personally identifiable information is removed from all replication material. Both papers' research plans received IRB approval before conducting their respective study.

Using tweets raises concerns about research reproducibility since a researcher cannot share more than 50,000 tweets per day. This restriction means that if the researcher has a dataset of 5 million tweets, it would take 100 days to transfer them to someone interested in reproduction. Relying on an individual to share tweets piecemeal does not encourage reproducible research, as the researcher will have to manually slice his or her data and remember to regularly share those tweets with interested parties. Interested parties may be dissuaded from inquiring in the first place, however, since the opportunity and coordination costs are not trivial.

Moreover, shared tweets cannot be provided via "non-automated means", and Twitter does not define that phrase. For example, suppose an academic publisher creates a script that automatically parses a tweet file into chunks of 50,000 tweets and tasks a staff member with sharing those chunks when requested. That script is an automated process, but the distribution mechanism (the staff member) is not. Now, suppose the publisher writes another script that e-mails those chunks to interested parties, but the staff member still has to initiate the sharing and e-mail scripts. Both solutions are less automated than allowing an interested party to initiate a series of downloads via a website interface, but the end result is the same. While it is clear that Twitter wants to impose costs on sharing data, sharing nonetheless exists over an indeterminate range in which those costs could fall.

The permitted workaround is to share the identification numbers for tweets, as an infinite number of those can be shared. This approach is easy for the original researcher and is the current best practice, but it requires greater computational skill for the interested party. Scripts provided in this Element (R script www.cambridge.org/download_file/949242 and Python script www.cambridge.org/download_file/929239), however, download tweets by their identification number.

Finally, researchers should carefully consider how to handle tweets created by bots. While the word "bot" has a nefarious connotation after the 2016 United States Presidential Election, a bot is simply an account which behaves following prescribed rules. It is quite common, for example, to see bots that tweet the weather, financial news, or sports scores. Spam accounts tend to be bots, and the earliest attempt to screen for bots was to flag any tweet from an account less than one day old or that contains at least three trending topics Kwak *et al.* (2010). Scholars soon realized that bots could also be used for political purposes, and they have been widely used by state and private political actors since at least 2011 (Wooley 2016).

As Twitter has evolved, so have bots, and bot detection has become an active area of research. One approach to identifying them is to use the source field in each tweet, as some sources are websites that allow customers to create and deploy bots (Forelle *et al.*, 2015). Other approaches rely on community detection algorithms, crowd-sourced manual labeling, or supervised machine learning (Ferrara et al. 2016b). The machine learning approach finds that "social bots", bots designed to behave like humans, retweet more than human accounts, have longer usernames, and are younger; they tweet, reply and mention others, and are retweeted less than human accounts (Ferrara et al. (2016b). The model on which Ferrara *et al.* (2016b) rely to analyze their sample is available through Indiana University's Observatory on Social Media's "Bot or Not?" project (Ferrara *et al.*, 2016a). Despite these advances in detection, bots continue to increase in sophistication and reach, and it is not clear that platforms will reach a point where they can eliminate bots. That bots require little financial capital makes their continued existence even more likely (Robertson, 2016; Bernstein, 2017).

While bots can be identified, their prevalence is an open question. During the 2016 United States Presidential Election, they were 14.4% of the top 50,000 users discussing Candidates Clinton and Trump and accounted for 18.45% of tweets about them (Ferrara and Bessi 2016). Lotan *et al.* (2011) find 6% of accounts in Egypt in January 2011 were bots, 8.4% in Tunisia. In my experience, bots are much less prevalent when samples are restricted to accounts with GPS coordinates or profile locations. Of accounts tweeting from Ukraine during six months in 2014, they were a negligible percentage, and the Kwak *et al.* (2010) filter found only about 3% of tweets during the Arab Spring were spam (Driscoll and Steinert-Threlkeld, 2017). The more esoteric a research topic and the more prevalent geotagged tweets are in a sample, the less likely are bots to constitute a worrisome presence. Finally, once identified, it is preferable to model bots' behavior and their effect on the larger social network than remove their tweets.

## 6.3   Is Twitter a Social Network or Media Platform?

Twitter is both a social network and a broadcast medium. It is certainly used by news organizations, politicians, celebrities, and corporations to broadcast messages, but it is also used by normal people engaging in activities that resemble how we think people behaved before they could document themselves on Twitter.

One of the most famous studies of Twitter, and one of the first, directly addresses the site's dual nature. Starting in June 2009, Haewoon Kwak and his coauthors crawled the site's 41.7 million profiles, 1.47 billion social ties, and 106 million tweets to study information diffusion on the network (Kwak *et al.*, 2010). Though their paper is titled, "What is Twitter, a Social Network or a News Media?", they do not directly answer this question; they show, however, that it is both, depending on the characteristics analyzed.

Like a social network, the distribution of followers conforms to a power-law distribution. The distribution of followings, however, does not, with noticeable irregularities at 20 and 2,000 followings (due to the design features of Twitter). Very few accounts follow more than 1,000 accounts, and those that do tend to be service oriented ones such as politicians and companies. Over 85% of trending topics are headline or persistent news, consistent with a media platform. On the other hand, a retweet reaches the same average number of users regardless of the number of followers of the tweet's author, consistent with a social network. Of users, 67.6%

are not followed by any of the accounts they follow, suggesting that these people use Twitter more to gather information than to engage socially. Twitter has a short diameter (4.12 average links between each account and all other accounts), which the authors interpret as support for the broadcast side of Twitter. Like social networks, users exhibit homophily, in this case with respect to their number of followers and time-zone. Finally, ranking accounts by their number of followers, their PageRank, and the number of times they are retweeted shows that the top 20 accounts in each tend to be news organizations or celebrities.

Though news organizations and celebrities dominate in terms of followers and retweets, that does not mean they dominate on other dimensions. For example, Steinert-Threlkeld (2017b) finds that those with the most followers did not drive protest mobilization during the Arab Spring. Even though those accounts will tweet about an upcoming or ongoing protest, the need for a critical mass of protestors means that it is the use of hashtags by those not at the top of the follower distribution that correlates with subsequent protest mobilization (Marwell *et al.*, 1988).

This result is in line with Barberá *et al.* (2015a). They find that communication around the 2014 Academy Awards and raising the United States' minimum wage resembles a broadcast network, while that for collective action has the same network dynamics identified in Steinert-Threlkeld (2017a). Gonzalez-Bailon *et al.* (2013) find four major types of Twitter users. Two of them – broadcasters (follow many fewer accounts than follow them, mentioned infrequently) and influentials (follow many fewer accounts than follow them, mentioned frequently) – are consistent with a media platform. The other two – common users (follow many more accounts than follow them, mentioned infrequently) and hidden influentials (follow many more accounts than follow them, mentioned frequently) – are consistent with a social network. Finally, a study of 1.8 billion tweets from four months in 2014 finds that only 0.8% of tweets are from news organizations, though some topics have up to 15% of their tweets coming from news organizations (Malik and Pfeffer, 2016). Individuals also commonly use

Twitter to engage in public conversations (Honeycutt and Herring, 2009; Boyd *et al.*, 2010).

Intriguingly, interactions accounts have with each other on Twitter parallel how humans are known to behave offline. Dunbar's Number is the observation that the number of social ties an animal can maintain is a function of the size of its neocortex in relation to the rest of the brain. For humans, this number is approximately 150 (Dunbar, 1992, 1995, 2011). Studying the reply and user mention behavior of 1.7 million networks, Bruno Goncalves *et al.* (2011) find that individuals on Twitter (bots were excluded) maintain between 100 and 200 connections (Gonçalves *et al.*, 2011). The 150 offline contacts humans maintain, however, exist in approximately three groups of increasing intimacy (Zhou *et al.*, 2005). Three social media datasets, two from Facebook and one from Twitter, replicate this relationship hierarchy, though they find evidence of four to five layers (Dunbar *et al.*, 2015).

Many papers' findings would not make sense if Twitter was not used as a social network. For example, the ability to recover ideology scores based on follower relationships, and to map those to voter records, would not be possible if users indiscriminately followed news organizations or political accounts (Barberá, 2015). Twitter users also exhibit less positive sentiment during working hours, consistent with social behaviors (Dodds *et al.*, 2011; Golder and Macy, 2011), and express greater positivity when they tweet further from their most common locations (Frank *et al.*, 2013). Exploiting the friendship paradox (your friends have more friends than you do because of the power-law distribution of friendship) allows you to detect emerging trends compared to monitoring a random sample of Twitter (Garcia-Herranz *et al.*, 2014). Governments and individuals monitor Twitter during natural disasters to maintain situational awareness (Vieweg *et al.*, 2010), and tweets even "detect" earthquakes (Sakaki *et al.*, 2010). Twitter has also been used to predict crime in Chicago (Gerber, 2014) and map linguistic communities in New York City (Mocanu *et al.*, 2013). These regularities would not occur if Twitter did not embody social behaviors.

Since behaviors on Twitter resemble a broadcast platform and a social network, researchers should work to keep individual and broadcast accounts analytically distinct. There are two approaches to identifying broadcast accounts, and individual accounts are then those outside of that set. The first approach is to manually search Twitter for a specific broadcast account; most organizations, like the *Los Angeles Times* or NBC News, have Twitter accounts. The researcher should then feed the account names to the GET users/lookup endpoint of the REST API and record the user identification number. That identification number should be used for subsequent calls to the API, e.g. if you want to follow that account from the streaming API. The second approach takes advantage of Twitter lists to quicken account identification. Twitter allows users to create publicly viewable lists of accounts, and users create lists around certain themes. For example, there are lists for French news and American cable television accounts. The best way to find these lists is via Google: in the search bar, type "site:twitter.com 'search term' list", e.g. "site:twitter.com 'France news'". Once the list name is identified, the list members can be manually recorded or downloaded via the GET lists/members.

For the foreseeable future, Twitter will continue to be the preferred data platform for social scientists, for two reasons. First, it remains a very large network. While it has not seen the growth envisioned at its initial public offering, its user base has grown. Controversies over its use for ISIS recruiting and the presence of racist and sexist harassers reflect real concerns, but those concerns have yet to affect the service's popularity. Second, no other platform provides data as easily as Twitter. Instagram could have threatened Twitter for researchers' loyalty, but the barriers created at the end of 2015 have taken away that prospect. Researchers interested in large datasets are now back to where they were in the mid-2000s: creating data by scraping blogs and news aggregators. Unless the researcher uses Twitter.[6]

---

[6] Facebook and Instagram are great sources of data, if you can convince them to work with you and are willing to risk their veto power.

The strongest growth prospect for Twitter is live events coverage. While people already turn to it to consume breaking news, and governments and news organizations use it to disseminate news, Twitter is working to expand into live video broadcasts. In 2016, it started to broadcast Thursday night National Football League games, and it livestreamed the 2016 United States Presidential debates (as did Facebook). It has also created a stand-alone application, Periscope, that lets anyone broadcast a live video from their phone. Because Periscope broadcasts are shown via Twitter, one possibility is to see if the number of video streams of certain events, like protests or riots, correlates with the actual number of attendees at those events. Researchers in media consumption have had to rely on self-reported surveys like Nielsen, so being able to observe in real time who observes broadcasts may present exciting new research opportunities.

These data are not a "revolution". Instead, they represent the next stage in the constant increase in data available to researchers. In the 1970s, cutting-edge empirical research consisted of descriptive statistics and basic regressions; using a computer required access to a mainframe and programming with punch cards. The 1980s and 1990s democratized computers for professionals, though data analysis programs did not become usable to those without programming knowledge until the 1990s.

The last two decades have witnessed the rise of digital communications data. Because these data are much cheaper to produce than human-created datasets, the amount of data available for analysis has expanded. This expansion has made previous approaches – aggregating data to the national or annual level, modeling data through graphical user interfaces such as Stata or SPSS, or loading an entire dataset at once, for example – often inadequate. Now, to stay at the forefront of data analysis, one needs to know some programming in order to interface with websites and data services, download data automatically, algorithmically clean and analyze data, and present these data in low-dimension environments. The skills are modern; the change is eternal.

# Glossary

**API**  Application Programming Interface. A standardized programming interface for accessing data or algorithms from a website.

**GDELT**  Global Database of Events, Location, and Tone. A dataset that reads newspapers in multiple languages and codes them for political events.

**GPS**  Global Positioning System. In this Element, "GPS coordinates" refers to the longitude and latitude that identifies the location from which a tweet was created.

**HTTP**  Hyptertext Transfer Protocol. The markup language computers use to talk to each other over the internet.

**ICEWS**  Integrated Conflict Early Warning System. A dataset that reads newspapers in multiple languages and codes them for political events.

**IRB**  Institutional Review Board. Bureaucracies located within universities which review any research involving human subjects.

**IP**  Internet Protocol. "IP Address" refers to the numerical identifier for a computer when communicating over the internet.

**JSON**  JavaScript Object Notation. A format for writing data that is easy for humans to read and compatible with data structures in most programming languages (dictionaries in Python, lists in R). It takes the form of key:value pairs that can be nested. The following example is a nested JSON object that shows names (keys) and the gender (nested key) and height (nested key) of each name: {'Zachary':{'Gender':'Male', 'Height':'Average'}, 'Jessica':{'Gender':'Female', 'Height':'Average'}}.

**NBA**  National Basketball Association. A professional sports league that figures prominently throughout examples.

**NoSQL**  Not Structured Query Language. A family of languages for retrieving data from databases that do not use table formats.

**RAM**  Random Access Memory. The working memory for a computer.

**REST API**  Representational State Transfer API. A standard set of operations to allow computers to exchange static information.

**SQL**  Structured Query Language. A language used for retrieving data from database tables.

**TCAT**  Twitter Collection and Analysis Toolkit. A series of tools for acquiring and analyzing Twitter data without programming knowledge.

**URL**  Uniform Resource Location. The address of a website.

**UTF-8**  Unicode Transformation Format. A standardized method for representing symbols, including emoji, across human languages.

# References

Acemoglu, Daron, Ahmed Tahoun, and Tarek A. Hassan (2014). "The Power of the Street: Evidence from Egypt's Arab Spring," NBER Working Paper No. 20665.

Adamic, Lada A. and Natalie Glance (2005). "The Political Blogosphere and the 2004 U.S. Election: Divided They Blog." In *Proceedings of the 3rd International Workshop on Link Discovery*, August 21-25, 2005, Chicago, IL, pp. 36-43.

Aday, Sean, Deen Freelon, Henry Farrell, Marc Lynch, and John Sides (2012). "New Media and Conflict After the Arab Spring." Technical Report, United States Institute of Peace, Washington, DC.

Aday, Sean, Henry Farrell, Marc Lynch, John Sides, John Kelly, and Ethan Zuckerman (2010). "Blogs and Bullets: New Media in Contentious Politics." Technical Report United States Institute of Peace, Washington, DC.

Analytics, Caerus (2015). "Open Event Data Alliance." phoenixdata.org.

Anastasopoulos, L. Jason, Dhruvil Badani, Crystal Lee, Shiry Ginosar, and Jake Williams (2016). "Photographic Home Styles in Congress: A Computer Vision Approach." http://arxiv.org/abs/1611.09942.

Asur, Sitaram and Bernardo A. Huberman (2010). "Predicting the Future with Social Media." In *2010 IEEE/WIC/ACM International Conference on Web Intelligence and Intelligent Agent Technology.* IEEE, pp. 492-99.

Bail, Christopher A. (2014). "The Cultural Environment: Measuring Culture with Big Data." *Theory and Society*, 43(3-4), 465-82.

Bakshy, Eytan, Solomon Messing, and Lada Adamic (2015). "Exposure to Ideologically Diverse News and Opinion on Facebook." *Sciencexpress*, 348(6239), 1160.

Barberá, Pablo (2013). "streamR." https://cran.r-project.org/web/packages/streamR/.

Barberá, Pablo (2014). "How Social Media Reduces Mass Political Polarization. Evidence from Germany, Spain, and the US." Paper prepared for the 2015 APSA Conference.

Barberá, Pablo (2015). "Birds of the Same Feather Tweet Together: Bayesian Ideal Point Estimation Using Twitter Data." *Political Analysis*, 23(August 2013), 76–91.

Barberá, Pablo, John T. Jost, Jonathan Nagler, Joshua A. Tucker, and Richard Bonneau (2015a). "Tweeting from Left to Right: Is Online Political Communication More Than an Echo Chamber?" *Psychological science*, 26(10),1531–42. www.ncbi.nlm.nih.gov/pubmed/26297377.

Barberá, Pablo, Ning Wang, Richard Bonneau, John T. Jost, Jonathan Nagler, Joshua Tucker, and Sandra González-Bailón (2015b). "The Critical Periphery in the Growth of Social Protests." *PloS ONE* 10(11), 1–15.

Barberá, Pablo, Richard Bonneau, Patrick Egan, John T. Jost, Jonathan Nagler, and Joshua Tucker (2014). "Leaders or Followers? Measuring Political Responsiveness in the US Congress Using Social Media Data." Prepared for delivery at the Annual Meeting of the American Political Science Association, August 28–31, 2014.

Bastos, Marco T., Dan Mercea, and Arthur Charpentier (2015). "Tents, Tweets, and Events: The Interplay between Ongoing Protests and Social Media." *Journal of Communication* 65(2), 320–350.

Beieler, John (2013). "A Tutorial on Deploying and Using Amazon Eleastic Cloud Compute Clusters." *The Political Methodologist* 20(2), 16–21.

Berger, Daniel, Shankar Kalyanaraman, and Sera Linardi (2014). "Violence and Cell Phone Communication: Behavior and Prediction in Cote d'Ivoire." Working paper.

Bergstrom, Kelly (2011). ""Don't Feed the Troll": Shutting Down Debate about Community Expectations on Reddit.com." *First Monday* 16(8).

Bernstein, Joseph (2017). "Never Mind the Russians, Meet the Bot King Who Helps Trump Win Twitter." www.buzzfeed.com/josephbernstein/from-utah-with-love?utm-term=.xqpxB9kRv#.tiDymBqG7.

Bhatia, Rahul (2016). "The Inside Story of Facebook's Biggest Setback." May 12. www.theguardian.com/technology/2016/may/12/facebook-free-basics-india-zuckerberg.

Bird, Steven, E. Klein, and E. Loper (2009). "*Natural Language Processing with Python: Analyzing Text with the Natural Language Toolkit.*" O'Reilly Media, Inc.

Blumenstock, J., G. Cadamuro, and R. On (2015). "Predicting Poverty and Wealth from Mobile Phone Metadata." *Science* 350(6264), 1073–1076.

Blumenstock, Joshua E (2011). "Using Mobile Phone Data to Measure the Ties Between Nations." In *Proceedings of the 2011 iConference*, pp. 195–202.

Blumenstock, Joshua E (2012). "Inferring Patterns of Internal Migration from Mobile Phone Call Records: Evidence from Rwanda." *Information Technology for Development* 18(2), 107–125.

Bollen, Johan, Huina Mao, and Xiaojun Zeng (2011). "Twitter Mood Predicts the Stock Market." *Journal of Computational Science* 2(1), 1–8.

Bond, Robert M., Christopher J. Fariss, Jason J. Jones, Adam D.I. Kramer, Cameron Marlow, Jaime E. Settle, and James H. Fowler (2012). "A 61-Million-Person Experiment in Social Influence and Political Mobilization." *Nature* 489(7415), 295–298.

Borge-Holthoefer, Javier, Walid Magdy, Kareem Darwish, and Ingmar Weber (2015). "Content and Network Dynamics behind Egyptian Political Polarization on Twitter." In *18th Conference on Computer-Supported Cooperative Work and Social Computing*, pp. 1–30.

Boschee, Elizabeth, Jennifer Lautenschlager, Sean O'Brien, Steve Shellman, James Starz, and Michael Ward (2015). "ICEWS Coded Event Data." http://dx.doi.org/10.7910/DVN/28075.

Bourlai, Elli and Susan C. Herring (2014). "Multimodal Communication on Tumblr: I Have So Many Feels!." In *Proceedings of the 2014 ACM Conference on Web Science*, pp. 171–175.

Boyd, Dannah, Scott Golder, and Gilad Lotan (2010). "Tweet, Tweet, Retweet: Conversational Aspects of Retweeting on Twitter." In *43rd Hawaii International Conference on System Sciences*. IEEE, pp. 1–10.

Budak, Ceren and Duncan Watts (2015). "Dissecting the Spirit of Gezi: Influence vs. Selection in the Occupy Gezi Movement." *Sociological Science* 2: 370–397.

Bury, Rhiannon, Ruth Deller, and Adam Greenwood (2013). "From Usenet to Tumblr: The Changing Role of Social Media." *Participations* 10(1), 299–318.

Catanese, Salvatore A, Pasquale De Meo, Emilio Ferrara, Giacomo Fiumara, and Alessandro Provetti (2011). "Crawling Facebook for Social Network Analysis Purposes." In *Proceedings of the International Conference on Web Intelligence, Mining and Semantics*. New York.

Cavnar, W. B. and J. M. Trenkle (1994). "n-Gram-Based Text Categorization." In *3rd Annual Symposium on Document Analysis and Information Retrieval*. Las Vegas, pp. 161–175.

Chang, Yi, Lei Tang, Yoshiyuki Inagaki, and Yan Liu (2014). "What is Tumblr: A Statistical Overview and Comparison." *SIGKDD Explorations* 16(1), 21–30.

Charles-Smith, Lauren E., Tera L. Reynolds, Mark A. Cameron, Mike Conway, Eric H. Y. Lau, Jennifer M. Olsen, Julie A. Pavlin, Mika Shigematsu, Laura C. Streichert, Katie J. Suda, and Courtney D. Corley (2015). "Using Social Media for Actionable Disease Surveillance and Outbreak Management: A Systematic Literature Review." *PLOS One* 10(10), e0139701.

Cheng, Zhiyuan, James Caverlee, and Kyumin Lee (2010). "You Are Where You Tweet: A Content-Based Approach to Geo-locating Twitter Users." In *ACM International Conference on Information and Knowledge Management*. Toronto.

Christia, Fotini, Leon Yao, Stephen Wittels, and Jure Leskovec (2015). "Yemen Calling: Seven Things Cell Data Reveal about Life in the Republic." *Foreign Affairs*. www.foreignaffairs.com/articles/yemen/2015-07-06/yemen-calling.

Conover, M.D., J. Ratkiewicz, M. Francisco, B. Goncalves, A. Flammini, and F. Menczer (2011). "Political Polarization on Twitter." In *Fifth International AAAI Conference on Weblogs and Social Media*, pp. 89–96.

Conover, Michael D., Bruno Gonçalves, Alessandro Flammini and Filippo Menczer (2012). "Partisan Asymmetries in Online Political Activity." *EPJ Data Science* 1(1), 1–19.

Conover, Michael D, Clayton Davis, Emilio Ferrara, Karissa McKelvey, Filippo Menczer, and Alessandro Flammini (2013). "The Geospatial Characteristics of a Social Movement Communication Network." *PloS one* 8(3), e55957.

Coppock, Alexander, Andrew Guess, and John Ternovski (2016). "When Treatments are Tweets: A Network Mobilization Experiment over Twitter." *Political Behavior* 38(1), 105–128. http://dx.doi.org/10.1007/s11109-015-9308-6.

Dalton, Russell J., Steven Greene, Paul Allen Beck, and Robert Huckfeldt (2002). "The Social Calculus of Voting: Interpersonal, Media, and Organizational Influences on Presidential Choices." *The American Political Science Review* 96(1), 57–73.

Davenport, Christian and Patrick Ball (2002). "Views to a Kill: Exploring the Implications of Source Selection in the Case of Guatemalan State Terror, 1977–1995)." *Journal of Conflict Resolution* 46(3), 427–450.

Diaz, Fernando, Michael Gamon, Jake Hofman, Emre Kiciman, and David Rothschild (2016). "Online and Social Media Data as a Flawed Continuous Panel Survey." *PLoS One* 11(1), e0145406.

Dodds, Peter Sheridan, Kameron Decker Harris, Isabel M. Kloumann, Catherine A. Bliss, and Christopher M. Danforth (2011). "Temporal Patterns of Happiness and Information in a Global Social Network: Hedonometrics and Twitter." *PLoS ONEcomput* 6(12), e26752.

Douglass, Rex W, David a Meyer, Megha Ram, David Rideout, and Dongjin Song (2015). "High Resolution Population Estimates from Telecommunications data." *EPJ Data Science* 4(1), 4.

Dowle, Matt, T Short, S Lianoglou, and A Srinivasan (2015). "data.table: Extension of data.frame." https://cran.r-project.org/web/packages/data.table/index.html.

Driscoll, Jesse and Zachary C. Steinert-Threlkeld (2017). "Structure, Agency, Hegemony, and Action: Ukrainian Nationalism in East Ukraine." Working paper.

Dunbar, R. I. M (2011). "Constraints on the Evolution of Social Institutions and Their Implications for Information Flow." *Journal of Institutional Economics* 7(03), 345–371. www.journals.cambridge.org/abstracES1744137410000366.

Dunbar, R. I. M. (1995). "Neocortex Size and Group Size In Primates: A Test of the Hypothesis." *Journal of Human Evolution* 28(3), 287–296.

Dunbar, R.I.M., Valerio Arnaboldi, Marco Conti, and Andrea Passarella (2015). "The Structure of Online Social Networks Mirrors Those in the Offline World." *Social Networks* 43: 39–47.

Eubank, Nicholas (2016). "Social Networks and the Political Salience of Ethnicity." Working paper.

Evans, Heather K., Victoria Cordova, and Savannah Sipole (2014). "Twitter Style: An Analysis of How House Candidates Used Twitter in Their 2012 Campaigns." *PS: Political Science & Politics* 47(02), 454–462.

Farrell, Henry (2012). "The Consequences of the Internet for Politics." *Annual Review of Political Science* 15(1), 35–52.

Ferrara, Emilio (2012). "A Large-Scale Community Structure Analysis in Facebook." *EPJ Data Science* 1(9), 1–30.

Ferrara, Emilio and Alessandro Bessi (2016). "Social Bots Distort the 2016 US Presidential Election Online Discussion." *First Monday* 21(11), 1–17.

Ferrara, Emilio, Onur Varol, Clayton Davis, Filippo Menczer, and Alessandro Flammini (2016a. "BotOrNot: A System to Evaluate Social

Bots." In *Proceedings of the 25th International Conference Companion on World Wide Web*, pp. 273–274.

Ferrara, Emilio, Onur Varol, Clayton Davis, Filippo Menczer, and Alessandro Flammini (2016b). "The Rise of Social Bots." *Communications of the ACM* 59(7), 96–104.

Ferrara, Emilio, Roberto Interdonato, and Andrea Tagarelli (2014). "Online Popularity and Topical Interests through the Lens of Instagram." *ACM Hypertext 2014*, 11.

Forelle, Michelle C, Philip N. Howard, Andres Monroy-Hernandez, and Saiph Savage (2015). "Political Bots and the Manipulation of Public Opinion in Venezuela." *SSRN Electronic Journal*, pp. 1–8.

Fowler, James and Zachary C. Steinert-Threlkeld (2016). "Online and Offline Activism in Egypt and Bahrain." Technical report United States Agency for International Development. www.iie.org/en/ Research-and-Publications/Publications-and-Reports/IIE-Bookstore/ DFG-UCSD-Publication#.V-MIM5MrKqA.

Frank, Morgan R, Lewis Mitchell, Peter Sheridan Dodds, and Christopher M Danforth (2013). "Happiness and the Patterns of Life: A Study of Geolocated Tweets." *Scientific Reports* 3:2625.

Freelon, Dean (2012). "Arab Spring Twitter Data Now Available (sort of)." http://dfreelon.org/2012/02/11/arab-spring-twitter-data-now-avail able-sort-of.

Gao, Qi, Fabian Abel, Geert-Jan Houben, and Yong Yu (2012). "A Comparative Study of Users' Mircroblogging Behavior on Sina Weibo and Twitter." In *Proceedings of International Conference on user Modelling and Personalization (UMAP2012)*, pp.88–101.

Garcia-Herranz, Manuel, Esteban Moro, Manuel Cebrian, Nicholas A. Christakis, and James H. Fowler (2014). "Using Friends as Sensors to Detect Global-Scale Contagious Outbreaks." *PloS ONE* 9(4), e92413.

Gayo-Avello, Daniel (2013). "A Meta-Analysis of State-of-the-Art Electoral Prediction from Twitter Data." *Social Science Computer Review* 31(6), 649–679.

Gentry, Jeff (2015). "twitteR." https://cran.r-project.org/web/packages/ twitteR/index.html.

Gerber, Matthew S. (2014). "Predicting Crime Using Twitter and Kernel Density Estimation." *Decision Support Systems* 61:115–125.

Gilbert, Eric (2013). "Widespread Underprovision on Reddit." In *Proceedings of the 2013 Conference on Computer Supported Cooperative Work*. New York: ACM Press p. 803.

Gjoka, Minas, U. C. Irvine, and Carter T. Butts (2010). "Walking in Facebook: A Case Study of Unbiased Sampling of OSNs." In *INFOCOM*. San Diego, CA.

Golder, Scott A. and Michael W. Macy (2011). "Diurnal and Seasonal Mood Vary with Work, Sleep, and Daylength across Diverse Cultures." *Science (New York, N.Y.)* 333(6051), 1878–81.

Golder, Scott A. and Michael W. Macy (2014). "Digital Footprints: Opportunities and Challenges for Online Social Research." *Annual Review of Sociology* 40(1), 129–152.

Gonçalves, Bruno, Nicola Perra, and Alessandro Vespignani (2011). "Modeling Users' Activity on Twitter Networks: Validation of Dunbar's Number." *PloS ONE* 6(8), e22656.

González-Bailón, Sandra, Javier Borge-Holthoefer, Alejandro Rivero, and Yamir Moreno (2011). "The Dynamics of Protest Recruitment through an Online Network." *Scientific Reports* 1:197.

Gonzalez-Bailon, Sandra, Javier Borge-Holthoefer, and Yamir Moreno (2013). "Broadcasters and Hidden Influentials in Online Protest Diffusion." *American Behavioral Scientist* 57(7), 943–965.

González-Bailón, Sandra, Ning Wang, Alejandro Rivero, Javier Borge-Holthoefer, and Yamir Moreno (2012). "Assessing the Bias in Communication Networks Sampled from Twitter."

Greenwood, Shannon, Andrew Perrin, and Maeve Duggan (2016). "Social Media Update 2016." Pew Research Center.

Grimmer, J. and B. M. Stewart (2013). "Text as Data: The Promise and Pitfalls of Automatic Content Analysis Methods for Political Texts." *Political Analysis* 21(3), 267–297.

Groshek, Jacob (2015). "Status Update on the BU-TCAT." www.jgroshek .org/blog/2015/8/17/status-update-on-the-bu-tcat.

Guan, Wanqiu, Haoyu Gao, Mingmin Yang, Yuan Li, Haixin Ma, Weining Qian, Zhigang Cao, and Xiaoguang Yang (2014). "Analyzing User Behavior of the Micro-Blogging Website Sina Weibo during Hot Social Events." *Physica A: Statistical Mechanics and its Applications* 395:340–351.

Halavais, Alexander (2011). "Social Science: Open Up Online Research." *Nature* 48, 174–175.

Hale, Scott A., Devin Gaffney, and Mark Graham (2011). "Where in the World Are You? Geolocation and Language Identification in Twitter." *The Professional Georgrapher* 66(4).

Hammond, Jesse and Nils B. Weidmann (2014). "Using Machine-Coded Event Data For The Micro-Level Study Of Political Violence." *Research & Politics* 1(2), 1–8.

Han, Bo and Timothy Baldwin (2011). "Lexical Normalisation of Short Text Messages: Makn Sens a #twitter." In *Proceedings of the 49th Annual Meeting of the Association for Computational Linguistics*. Porland: Association for Computational Linguistics, pp. 368–378.

Hassid, Jonathan (2012). "Safety Valve or Pressure Cooker? Blogs in Chinese Political Life." *Journal of Communication* 62(2), 212–230.

Hayden, Erika Check (2013). "Guidance Issued for US Internet Research: Institutional Review Boards May Need to Take a Closer Look at Some Types of Online Research." www.nature.com/news/guidance-issued-for-us-internet-research-1.12860.

Hecht, Brent, Lichan Hong, Bongwon Suh, and Ed H. Chi (2011). "Tweets from Justin Bieber's Heart: The Dynamics of the Location Field in User Profiles." In *ACM Conference on Human Factors in Computing Systems*. Number Figure 1 Vancouver:.

Hemphill, Libby, Jahna Otterbacher, and Matthew Shapiro (2013). "What's Congress Doing on Twitter?" In *Proceedings of the 2013 conference on Computer Supported Cooperative Work*, pp. 877–886.

Henrich, Joseph, Steven J. Heine, and Ara Norenzayan (2010). "The Weirdest People in the World." *The Behavioral and Brain Sciences* 33(2–3), 61–83; discussion 83–135.

Hochman, Nadav and Lev Manovich (2013). "Zooming into an Instagram City: Reading the Local Through Social Media." *First Monday* 18(7), 1–37.

Honeycutt, Courtenay and Susan C. Herring (2009). "Beyond Microblogging: Conversation and Collaboration via Twitter." In *Proceedings of the 42nd Hawaii International Conference on System Sciences*, pp. 1–10.

Hu, Yuheng, Lydia Manikonda, and Subbarao Kambhampati (2014). "What we Instagram: A First Analysis of Instagram Photo Content and User Types." In *Proceedings of the Eight International AAAI Conference on Weblogs and Social Media*, pp. 595–598.

Jones, Harvey and Jose Hiram Soltren (2005). "Facebook: Threats to privacy." *Project MAC: MIT Project on Mathematics and Computing* 1:1–76.

Jungherr, Andreas (2014). "Twitter in Politics: A Comprehensive Literature Review."

Kallus, Nathan (2013). "Predicting Crowd Behavior with Big Public Data." In *23rd International Conference on World Wide Web*.

Kalyvas, Stathis N (2004). *The Urban Bias in Research on Civil Wars*. Vol. 13.

Kaneko, Takamu and Keiji Yanai (2013). "Visual Event Mining from Geo-Tweet Photos." In *IEEE International Conference on Multimedia and Expo Workshops*, pp. 1–6.

King, Gary, Jennifer Pan, and Margaret E. Roberts (2014). "Reverse-Engineering Censorship in China: Randomized Experimentation and Participant Observation." *Science* 345(6199), 1–10.

King, Gary, Jennifer Pan, and Margaret E. Roberts (2016). "How the Chinese Government Fabricates Social Media Posts for Strategic Distraction, not Engaged Argument." http://gking.harvard.edu/50c?platform=hootsuite.

Kramer, Adam D.I., Jamie E. Guillory, and Jeffrey T. Hancock (2014). "Experimental evidence of massive-scale emotional contagion through social networks." In *Proceedings of the National Academy of Sciences* 111(24), 8788–8790.

Kulshrestha, Juhi, Farshad Kooti, Ashkan Nikravesh, and Krishna P Gummadi (2012). "Geographic Dissection of the Twitter Network." In *Proceedings of the Sixth International AAAI Conference on Weblogs and Social Media*, pp. 202–209.

Kwak, Haewoon, Changhyun Lee, Hosung Park, and Sue Moon (2010). "What Is Twitter, a Social Network or a News Media?" In *International World Wide Conference*. Raleigh: ACM Press, pp. 591–600.

Lake, Ronald La Due and Robert Huckfeldt (1998). "Social Capital, Social Networks, and Political Participation." *Political Psychology* 19(3), 567–584.

Lakkaraju, Himabindu, Julian J. McAuley, and Jure Leskovec (2013). "What's in a Name? Understanding the Interplay between Titles, Content, and Communities in Social Media." In *International Conference on Web and Social Media*.

Lang, Duncan Temple and the CRAN team (2016). RCurl: General Network Client Interface for R. R package version 1.95-4.8. https://CRAN.R-project.org/package=RCurl

Larson, Jennifer M., Jonathan Nagler, Jonathan Ronen, and Joshua A. Tucker (2016). "Social Networks and Protest Participation: Evidence from 130 Million Twitter Users." Working paper.

Lazer, David, Devon Brewer, Nicholas Christakis, James Fowler, and Gary King (2009). "Life in the Network: The Coming Age of Computational Social Science." *Science* 323(5915), 721–723.

Leetaru, Kalev H., Shaowen Wang, Guofeng Cao, Anand Padmanabhan, and Eric Shook (2013). "Mapping the Global Twitter Heartbeat: The Geography of Twitter." *First Monday* 18(5–6), 1–33.

Leetaru, Kalev and Philip Schrodt (2013). "GDELT: Global Data on Events, Language, and Tone, 1979–2012." *International Studies Association Annual Conference*.

Lewis, Kevin, Jason Kaufman, Marco Gonzalez, Andreas Wimmer, and Nicholas Christakis (2008). "Tastes, Ties, and Time: A New Social Network Dataset Using Facebook.com." *Social Networks* 30(4), 330–342. http://linkinghub.elsevier.com/retrieve/pii/S0378873308000385.

Lin, Chengfeng, Jianhua He, Yi Zhou, Xiaokang Yang, Kai Chen, and Li Song (2013). "Analysis and Identification of Spamming Behaviors in Sina Weibo Microblog." In *Proceedings of the 7th Workshop on Social Network Mining and Analysis* 13: 1–9.

Llorente, Alejandro, Manuel Garcia-Herranz, Manuel Cebrian, and Esteban Moro (2014). "Social media fingerprints of unemployment." http://arxiv.org/abs/1411.3140.

Lotan, Gilad, Mike Ananny, Devin Gaffney, Danah Boyd, Ian Pearce, and Erhardt Graeff (2011). "The Revolutions Were Tweeted: Information Flows During the 2011 Tunisian and Egyptian Revolutions Web." *International Journal of Communications* 5:1375–1406.

Lucas, Christopher, Richard A. Nielsen, Margaret E. Roberts, Brandon M. Stewart, Alex Storer, and Dustin Tingley (2015). "Computer-Assisted Text Analysis for Comparative Politics." *Political Analysis* 23(2), 254–277.

Malik, Momin M., Constantine Nakos, Hemank Lamba, and Jiirgen Pfeffer (2015). "Population Bias in Geotagged Tweets." In *9th International AAAI Conference on Weblogs and Social Media*. Oxford.

Malik, Momin M. and Jurgen Pfeffer (2016). "A Macroscopic Analysis of News Content in Twitter." *Digital Journalism* 0811(May), 1–25.

Manning, Christopher D. and Hinrich Schutze (1999). *Foundations of Statistical Natural Language Processing*. Cambridge, MA: Massachusetts Institute of Technology.

Marwell, Gerald, Pamela E. Oliver, and Ralph Prahl (1988). "Social Networks and Collective Action: A Theory of the Critical Mass." *American Journal of Sociology* 94(3), 502–534.

Masad, David (2013). "Studying the Syrian Civil War with GDELT." *The Monkey Cage.* http://themonkeycage.org/2013/07/09/how-computers-can-help-us-track-violent-conflicts-including-right-now-in-syria/.

McAdam, Doug (1986). "Recruitment to High-Risk Activism: The Case of Freedom Summer." *American Journal of Sociology* 92(1), 64–90.

McGrath, Ryan (2015). "twython." https://twython.readthedocs.io/en/latest/.

McKinney, Wes (2015). "pandas." *http://pandas.pydata.org/*.

Metternich, Nils W., Cassy Dorff, Max Gallop, Simon Weschle, and Michael D. Ward (2013). "Antigovernment Networks in Civil Conflicts: How Network Structures Affect Conflictual Behavior." *American Journal of Political Science* 57(4).

Mislove, Alan, Sune Lehmann, Yong-Yeol Ahn, Jukka-Pekka Onnela, and J. Niels Rosenquist. 2011). "Understanding the Demographics of Twitter Users." In *Proceedings of the Fifth International AAI Conference on the Weblogs and Social Media,* pp. 554–557.

Mocanu, Delia, Andrea Baronchelli, Nicola Perra, Alessandro Vespignani, Bruno Goncalves, and Qian Zhang (2013). "The Twitter of Babel: Mapping World Languages through Microblogging Platforms." *PLOS One* 8(4), e61981.

Morstatter, Fred, Jurgen Pfeffer, Kathleen M. Carley, and Huan Liu (2013). "Is the Sample Good Enough? Comparing Data from Twitter's Streaming API with Twitter's Firehose." In *Association for the Advancement of Artificial Intelligence.*

Mueller, Andreas (2015). "scikit-learn." http://scikit-learn.org/stable/.

Munger, Kevin (2016). "Tweetment Effects on the Tweeted: Experimentally Reducing Racist Harassment." *Political Behavior,* pp. 1–21.

Mustafaraj, E. and Pt Metaxas (2010). "From Obscurity to Prominence in Minutes: Political Speech and Real-Time Search." In *WebSci10: Extending the Frontiers of Society On-Line.* p. 317. http://repository.wellesley.edu/computersciencefaculty/9/.

Nguyen, Dong, Rilana Gravel, Dolf Trieschnigg, and Theo Meder (2013). ""How Old Do You Think I Am ?: A Study of Language and Age in Twitter." Proceedings of the Seventh International AAAI Conference on Weblogs and Social Media.

Nickerson, David W. (2008). "Is Voting Contagious? Evidence from Two Field Experiments." *American Political Science Review* 102(01), 49–57.

Onuch, Olga (2015). "EuroMaidan Protests in Ukraine: Social Media Versus Social Networks." *Problems of Post-Communism* 62(4), 217–235.

Opp, Karl-Dieter and Christiane Gern (1993). "Dissident Groups, Personal Networks, and Spontaneous Cooperation: The East German Revolution of 1989." *American Sociological Review* 58(5), 659–680.

Poblete, Barbara, Ruth Garcia, Marcelo Mendoza, and Alejandro Jaimes (2011). "Do All Birds Tweet the Same? Characterizing Twitter Around the World Categories and Subject Descriptors." In *The 21st ACM Conference on Information and Knowledge Management*, pp. 1025–1030.

Qu, Yan, Chen Huang, Pengyi Zhang, and Jun Zhang (2011). "Microblogging after a Major Disaster in China: A Case Study of the 2010 Yushu Earthquake." In *Computer Supported Cooperative Work*. Hangzhou, China, pp. 25–34.

Rahimi, Babak (2011). "The Agonistic Social Media: Cyberspace in the Formation of Dissent and Consolidation of State Power in Postelection Iran." *The Communication Review* 14(3), 158–178.

Ramakrishnan, Naren, Chang-tien Lu, Bert Huang, Aravind Srinivasan, Khoa Trinh, and Lise Getoor (2014). "Beating the News' with EMBERS: Forecasting Civil Unrest using Open Source Indicators." In *Proceedings of the 20th ACM SIGKDD International Conference on Knowledge Discovery and Data Mining*. New York City: ACM Press, pp. 1799–1808.

Ratkiewicz, Jacob, Michael D. Conover, Mark Meiss, Bruno Goncalves, Alessandro Flamini, and Filippo Menczer (2011). "Detecting and Tracking Political Abuse in Social Media." In *International Conference on Web and Social Media*, pp. 297–304.

Reich, Stephanie M., Kaveri Subrahmanyam, and Guadalupe Espinoza (2012). "Friending, IMing, and hanging out Face-to-Face: Overlap in Adolescents' Online and Offline Social Networks." *Developmental Psychology* 48(2), 356–368.

Reuter, Ora John and David Szakonyi (2013). "Online Social Media and Political Awareness in Authoritarian Regimes." *British Journal of Political Science*, pp. 1–23.

Roberts, Margaret E., Brandon M. Stewart, Dustin Tingley, Christopher Lucas, Jetson Leder-Luis, Shana Kushner Gadarian, Bethany Albertson, and David G. Rand (2014). "Structural Topic Models for Open-Ended Survey Responses." *American Journal of Political Science* 58(4), 1064–1082.

Robertson, Jordan (2016). "How to Hack an Election." Bloomberg Businessweek. www.bloomberg.com/features/2016-how-to-hack-an-election/.

Sakaki, Takeshi, Makoto Okazaki, and Yutaka Matsuo (2010). "Earthquake Shakes Twitter Users: Real-time Event Detection by Social Sensors." In *International World Wide Web Conference*, pp. 851–860.

Seabold, Skipper and Josepf Perktold (2014). "statstools." https://pypi.python.org/pypi/statsmodels.

Shweder, Richard A. and Richard E. Nisbett (2017). "Long-Sought Research Deregulation Is Upon Us: Don't Squander the Moment." *The Chronicle for Higher Education*, 12 March 2017.

Silva, Thiago H., Pedro O.S. Vaz De Melo, Jussara M. Almeida, Juliana Salles, and Antonio A. F. Loureiro (2013). "A Picture of Instagram Is Worth More than a Thousand Words: Workload Characterization and Application." In *2013 IEEE International Conference on Distributed Computing in Sensor Systems*, pp. 123–132.

Sloan, Luke and Jeffrey Morgan (2015). "Who Tweets with Their Location? Understanding the Relationship Between Demographic Characteristics and the Use of Geoservices and Geotagging on Twitter." *PLoS ONE* 10 (11), 1–15.

Sloan, Luke, Jeffrey Morgan, Pete Burnap, and Matthew Williams (2015). "Who Tweets? Deriving the Demographic Characteristics of Age, Occupation and Social Class from Twitter User Meta-Data." *PLoS ONE* 10(3), 1–20.

Social, We Are (2016). "Leading Social Networks Worldwide as of April 2016, Ranked by Number of Active Users." www.statista.com/statistics/272014/global-social-networks-ranked-by-number-of-users/.

Solon, Olivia (2016). "How Facebook Plans to Take Over the World." www.theguardian.com/technology/2016/apr/23/facebook-global-takeover-f8-conference-messenger-chatbots.

Sriram, Bharath, David Fuhry, Engin Demir, Hakan Ferhatosmanoglu, and Murat Demirbas (2010). "Short Text Classification in Twitter to Improve Information Filtering." In *Proceedings of the 33rd international ACM SIGIR conference on Research and development in information retrieval – SIGIR '10*. New York: ACM Press, pp. 841–842.

Starbird, Kate and Ley Palen (2010). "Pass It On?: Retweeting in Mass Emergency." In *Information Systems for Crisis Response and Management*. December 2004, Seattle, pp. 1–10.

Stefanidis, Anthony, Andrew Crooks, and Jacek Radzikowski (2011). "Harvesting Ambient Geospatial Information from Social Media Feeds." *GeoJournal* 78(2), 319-338.

Steinert-Threlkeld, Zachary C (2016). "Replication Data for: Longitudinal Network Centrality Using Incomplete Data." http://dx.doi.org/10.7910/DVN/KKWB4A.

Steinert-Threlkeld, Zachary C (2017a). "Longitudinal Network Analysis with Incomplete Data." *Political Analysis*. DOI: https://doi.org/10.1017/pan.2017.6.

Steinert-Threlkeld, Zachary C (2017b). "Spontaneous Collective Action: Peripheral Mobilization during the Arab Spring." *American Political Science Review* 111(02), 379-403.

Steinert-Threlkeld, Zachary C., Delia Mocanu, Alessandro Vespignani, and James Fowler (2015). "Online Social Networks and Offline Protest." *EPJ Data Science* 4(1), 19.

Stone, Biz (2010). "Tweet Preservation." https://blog.twitter.com/2010/tweet-preservation.

Suh, Bongwon, Lichan Hong, Peter Pirolli, and Ed H. Chi (2010). "Want to be Retweeted? Large Scale Analytics on Factors Impacting Retweet in Twitter Network." In *IEEE Second International Conference on Social Computing*, pp. 177-184.

Sun, Shengyun, Hongyan Liu, Jun He, and Xiaoyong Du (2013). "Detecting Event Rumors on Sina Weibo Automatically." In *Web Technologies and Applications*, pp. 120-131.

Tucker, Joshua A., Jonathan Nagler, Megan MacDuffee Metzger, Pablo Barberá, Duncan Penfold-Brown, and Richard Bonneau (2016). "Big Data, Social Media, and Protest: Foundations for a Research Agenda." In R. Michael Alvarez, *Computational Social Science: Discovery and Prediction*. Cambridge: Cambridge University Press, chapter 7, pp. 199-224.

Tufekci, Zeynep (2014). "Big Questions for Social Media Big Data: Representativeness, Validity and Other Methodological Pitfalls Preprint." In *Proceedings of the 8th International AAAI Conference on Weblogs and Social Media*. Ann Arbor.

Tufekci, Zeynep and Christopher Wilson (2012). "Social Media and the Decision to Participate in Political Protest: Observations From Tahrir Square." *Journal of Communication* 62(2), 363-379.

Tufekci, Zeynep and Deen Freelon (2013). "Introduction to the Special Issue on New Media and Social Unrest." *American Behavioral Scientist* 57(7), 843–847.

Tumasjan, Andranik, Timm O. Sprenger, Philipp G. Sandner, and Isabell M. Welpe (2010). "Predicting Elections with Twitter: What 140 Characters Reveal about Political Sentiment." In *Association for the Advancement of Artificial Intelligence*, pp. 178–185.

Twitter (2016). "Selected Company Metrics and Financials." Technical Report. http://files.shareholder.com/downloads/AMDA-2F526X/ 5527362927x0x935049/05E6E71E-D609-4A17-A8BD-B621324A950D/ TWTR_2016_Annual_Report.pdf.

Ugander, Johan, Brian Karrer, Lars Backstrom, and Cameron Marlow (2011). "The Anatomy of the Facebook Social Graph." arXiv:1111.4503.

*Update on the Twitter Archive At the Library of Congress* (2013). *Technical Report*, January, Library of Congress Washington, DC.

Valkanas, George, Ioannis Katakis, Dimitrios Gunopulos, and Antony Stefanidis (2014). "Mining Twitter Data with Resource Constraints." In *2014 International Joint Conferences on Web Intelligence (WI) and Intelligent Agent Technologies (IAT)*. IEEE, pp. 157–164.

Vieweg, Sarah, Amanda L. Hughes, Kate Starbird, and Leysia Palen (2010). "Microblogging During Two Natural Hazards Events: What Twitter May Contribute to Situational Awareness." In *Human Factors in Computing Systems*. Atlanta, pp. 1079–1088.

Ward, Brian (2014). "TCAT: The New Twitter Modeling Tool for Visualizing Social Media Data." http://painepublishing.com/measure mentadvisor/pretty-pictures-new-twitter-modeling-tool-can-make- social-media-data-tangible-actionable/.

Weber, Ingmar, Venkata R. Kiran Garimella, and Alaa Batayneh (2013). "Secular vs. Islamist Polarization in Egypt on Twitter." In *IEEE/ACM International Conference on Advances in Social Networks Analysis and Mining*, pp. 290–297.

Weidmann, Nils B (2014). "On the Accuracy of Media-based Conflict Event Data." *Journal of Conflict Resolution* 59(6), 1129–1149. http:// jcr.sagepub.com/cgi/doi/10.1177/0022002714530431.

Weidmann, Nils B. and Michael D. Ward (2010). "Predicting Conflict in Space and Time." *Journal of Conflict Resolution* 54(6), 883–901, http:// jcr.sagepub.com/cgi/doi/10.1177/0022002710371669.

Wilson, R. E., S. D. Gosling, and L. T. Graham (2012). "A Review of Facebook Research in the Social Sciences." *Perspectives on Psychological Science* 7(3), 203–220.

Woolley, Samuel C (2016). "Automating Power: Social Bot Interference in Global Politics." *First Monday* 21(4), 1–13.

Xu, Jiejun, Tsai-Ching Lu, Ryan Compton, and David Allen (2014). "Civil Unrest Prediction: A Tumblr-Based Exploration." In William G. Kennedy, Nitin Agarwal, and Shanchieh Jay Yang *Social Computing, Behavioral-Cultural Modeling and Prediction*, Vol. 8393. Springer International Publishing, pp. 403–411.

Yardi, Sarita and Danah Boyd (2010). "Tweeting from the Town Square: Measuring Geographic Local Networks." In *Fourth International AAAI Conference on Weblogs and Social Media*, pp. 194–201.

Yazdani, Mehrdad and Lev Manovich (2015). "Predicting Social Trends from Non-Photographic Images on Twitter." In *Proceedings – 2015 IEEE International Conference on Big Data, IEEE Big Data 2015*, pp. 1653–1660.

Yu, Louis Lei, Sitaram Asur, and Bernardo A. Huberman (2012). "Artificial Inflation: The Real Story of Trends and Trend-Setters in Sina Weibo." In *Privacy, Security, Risk and Trust (PASSAT), 2012 International Conference on and 2012 International Confernece on Social Computing (SocialCom)*, pp. 514–519.

Zamal, Faiyaz Al, Wendy Liu, and Derek Ruths (2012). "Homophily and Latent Attribute Inference: Inferring Latent Attributes of Twitter Users from Neighbors." In *Proceedings of the Sixth International AAAI Conference on Weblogs and Social Media*, pp. 387–90.

Zeitzoff, Thomas (2011). "Using Social Media to Measure Conflict Dynamics: An Application to the 2008–2009 Gaza Conflict." *Journal of Conflict Resolution* 55(6), 938–69.

Zeitzoff, Thomas (2016). "Does Social Media Influence Conflict? Evidence from the 2012 Gaza Conflict." *Journal of Conflict Resolution*, forthcoming. https://doi.org/10.1177/0022002716650925.

Zeitzoff, Thomas, John Kelly, and Gilad Lotan (2015). "Using Social Media to Measure Foreign Policy Dynamics: An Empirical Analysis of the Iranian–Israeli Confrontation (2012-13)." *Journal of Peace Research* 52(3), 368–383.

Zheludev, Ilya, Robert Smith, and Tomaso Aste (2014). "When Can Social Media Lead Financial Markets?" *Scientific Reports* 4(4213).

Zhou, W.-X., D. Sornette, Russell A. Hill, and R. I. M. Dunbar (2005). "Discrete Hierarchical Organization of Social Group Sizes." *Proceedings. Biological Sciences/The Royal Society* 272(1561). 439–444.

Zickuhr, Kathryn (2013). "Location-Based Services." *Pew Research Center's Internet & American Life* 51 (September), 65–69, www.pewinternet.org/2013/09/12/location-based-services/.

Zimmer, Michael (2015). "The Twitter Archive at the Library of Congress: Challenges for Information Practice and Information Policy". *First Monday* 20(7), 1–12.